ecologica

THE FRENCH LIST

ecologica

ANDRÉ GORZ

TRANSLATED BY CHRIS TURNER

LONDON NEW YORK CALCUTTA

Seagull Books, 2018

First published in France as *Ecologica* by André Gorz
Copyright © Editions Galilée, 2008

English language translation copyright © Chris Turner, 2010
First published in English by Seagull Books, 2010

ISBN   978 0 8574 2 575 1

British Library Cataloguing-in-Publication Data
A catalogue record for this book is available
from the British Library

Typeset by Seagull Books, Calcutta, India
Printed at Leelabati Printers, Calcutta India

CONTENTS

POLITICAL ECOLOGY, AN ETHICS OF LIBERATION

MARC ROBERT: *From the publication of the autobiographical novel,* The Traitor (1958), *with a preface by Jean-Paul Sartre, to your involvement in political ecology, what, for you, have been the most important encounters and influences?*

ANDRÉ GORZ: The great encounters and influences in my life? There was Sartre, of course, whose work from 1943 onwards had a formative role for me over a 20-year period. There was Illich, who, from 1971, provided me with food for thought for five years. But the most important influences aren't necessarily those of the most important people. Jean-Marie Vincent,[1] who published relatively little, initiated me into the Marx of the *Grundrisse*[2] as early as 1959. He introduced me to Italian theorists, who led me to others. In the 1990s, through his journal *Futur Antérieur*, he convinced me I had to revise some of my ideas.[3] Two years ago, following an interview on my book *L'Immatériel*[4] for a German newspaper, I met a 'hacker'[5] by the name of Stefen Meretz, co-founder of Oekonux,[6] an organization that explores, with laudable honesty, the difficulties posed by an exit from capitalism through practice, through one's mode of living, desiring and thinking.

But from 1947 to the present, the strongest, most constant influence has been that of my partner 'Dorine, without whom nothing would be.' She is the one who showed me that it wasn't impossible to love and be loved, to feel, live and have confidence in oneself. We've grown and developed through each other and for each other. Without her, I'd probably never have come to accept myself. Without Sartre, I probably wouldn't have found the tools for conceptualizing and transcending what my family and history had made me. The moment I discovered *Being and Nothingness* (1943), I felt that what Sartre said of the human ontological condition matched my experience. From earliest childhood, I'd experienced all the 'existentials': anxiety, boredom, the certainty of purposelessness, of not meeting other people's expectations, of not being able to be understood by them. In short, every human subject's experience of contingency, unjustifiability and loneliness.

Can you tell us more about these links between existentialism and ecology, between morality, ethics and ecology?

The question of the subject has remained central for me, as it was for Sartre, in the following way. We are born to ourselves as subjects—in other words, as subjects irreducible to what other people and society ask us to be and allow us to be. Our upbringing, socialization, education and integration teach us, subsequently, to be Others among Others, to deny that non-socializable part of ourselves that is the experience of being a subject, and channel our lives and desires into pre-ordained pathways, to merge with the roles and functions that the social megamachine demands we fulfil.

It's these roles and functions that define our identity as Other. They go beyond what each of us can be by himself. They exempt us—or even prevent us—from existing by ourselves, from asking questions about the meaning of our actions and taking responsibility for them. It's not 'I' who acts, but the automated logic of social systems that works through me as Other, that makes me participate in the production and reproduction of the social megamachine. That logic is the real subject. And the dominant social strata suffer its domination, as much as do the dominated. The dominant dominate only insofar as they serve it as loyal functionaries. It's only in the interstices of this logic, its misfirings and margins, that autonomous subjects emerge, through whom moral questions may be posed. At the origin of such questions, there's always that founding act of the subject which consists in rebellion against what society makes me do or undergo. Alain Touraine, who studied Sartre in his youth, puts this very well: 'The subject is always a bad subject,' resisting power and rules, 'resisting the total apparatus known as society'.[7] Hence, the question of the subject is the same thing as the question of morality. It lies at the foundation of both ethics and politics, since it necessarily calls into question all the forms and means of domination or, in other words, all the things that prevent people from behaving as subjects and pursuing the free flourishing of their individuality as their common goal.

It's been clear for 170 years that we're dominated in our work. But not that we're dominated in our needs, desires, thoughts and self-images. This was already present in *The Traitor* and is redeveloped in almost all my later writings. It was through this theme, through the critique of the model of affluent consumption, that I became an ecologist before the term even existed. My starting point was an article that appeared in an American weekly around 1954. It explained that, if America's productive capacity was to make a return on investment, consumption would have to grow by at least 50 per cent in the next eight years, but that people were quite incapable of defining what their additional 50 per cent consumption would consist of. It was up to the advertising and marketing experts to summon up new needs, desires and fantasies on the part of consumers, to deck out even the most trivial commodities with symbols that would increase the demand for them. Capitalism needed people to have greater needs. But, more than this, it had to be able to shape and develop those needs in the way most profitable for capitalism, by incorporating a maximum of superfluity into the needful, by speeding up obsolescence, by reducing product durability, by forcing people to meet their tiniest needs with the greatest possible degree of consumption and by eliminating collective goods and services (trams and trains, for example) and replacing them with individual purchases. Consumption had to be individualized and private, so that it could be subordinated to the interests of capital.

Starting out from the critique of capitalism, we arrive then, inevitably, at political ecology, which, with its indispensable critical theory of needs, leads in turn to a deeper and more radical critique of capitalism. So I wouldn't say that there's a morality of ecology, but rather that the ethical demand for the emancipation of the subject implies the theoretical and practical critique of capitalism, of which political ecology is an essential dimension. If, on the other hand, you start out from the ecological imperative, you may just as easily arrive at a Green Pétainism, an eco-fascism or a naturalistic communitarianism as you may at a radical anti-capitalism. Ecology has its full critical and ethical impact only if the devastation of the Earth and the destruction of the natural foundations of life are understood as the consequences of a mode of production; and if that mode of production demands the maximization of output and has recourse to technologies that violate biological equilibria. I contend, then, that the critique of the technologies in which the domination of human beings and nature is embodied is one of the essential dimensions of an ethics of liberation.

My interest in the critique of technology owes a great deal to my reading of Sartre's *Critique of Dialectical Reason* in 1960, to 10 days spent visiting factories in East Germany in that same period in a vain search for the seeds of workers' power; and then to the discovery, in 1971 or '72, of Illich, who had given the title *Retooling Society* to the first draft of his book *Tools for Conviviality*.[8] Illich drew a distinction between two types of technologies: those he termed 'convivial', which increase the field of autonomy, and the heteronomous type which restrict or suppress it. I called these 'open technologies' and 'locking technologies'. Open technologies are ones that promote communication, cooperation and interaction, like the telephone or, among current technologies, free networks and software. 'Locking technologies' are those that enslave the user, programme her operations or monopolize the supply of a product or service.

The worst of the 'locking technologies' are, obviously, the megatechnologies, monuments to the domination of nature, which deprive human beings of their living environment and submit them to their domination. In addition to all its other faults, it was the way nuclear technology radiates totalitarianism through society, in the form of secrets, lies and violence, that led me to campaign against it for 10 years.

In this radical critique of capitalism, there's a passage through Communism and then, later, its abandonment?

Écologie et liberté (1977), which was a kind of Afterword to *Écologie et Politique,*[9] began with this statement: 'Socialism is no better than capitalism if it does not change tools.' The next book, *Farewell to the Working Class* (1980), went further in this same direction. It argued that, as a result of the division, organization and hierarchization of work that they either require or make possible, capitalism's means of production are means of domination. The working class can no more seize the means of production, by which it's structured, functionally divided and dominated, than soldiers can seize the army, without changing its rules and mode of organization from top to bottom. If it took control of the means of production without altering them radically, it would end up reproducing the same system of domination—as occurred in the Soviet-bloc countries. This is, incidentally, all mentioned in passing in the *Grundrisse*.[10] *Farewell to the Working Class* was in no sense a critique of Communism. Far from it. The butt of my attack were the Maoists with their primitivistic cult of a mythic proletariat and their pretensions of implementing, in an industrialized, urbanized country, the strategy of land-grabs invented by Mao for the Chinese peasantry. It is also a scathing critique of the social democratization of capitalism, which is what vulgar Marxism actually amounted to, and of the glorification of wage labour. 'Beyond Socialism'—that was the book's subtitle[11]—

there's Communism, which is its culmination, or, failing that, the horrible mess we're in today. But Communism is neither full employment nor a wage for everyone, but the elimination of work in the socially and historically specific form it has in capitalism. That is to say, it is the elimination of work-as-employment, work-as-commodity. With *Farewell to the Working Class*, I moved on to the critique of work. It was a book that also had some foolish blunders in it (including the idea of a 'sphere of autonomy'), but there was more to it than that. The critique of work was still central in *Reclaiming Work: Beyond the Wage-Based Society*.[12]

The critique of the division of labour becomes highly problematical with the increase in the part played by knowledge in production, with cooperation in the creation of wealth, and with 'virtuoso work'. Your latest work, L'Immatériel, *attempts to think through these changes.*[13]

L'Immatériel is the by-product of a report to an international conference on the so-called knowledge society, as seen from the Left.[14] What interested me in that, first of all, is that knowledge and information are, of their essence, common goods which belong to everyone and cannot, therefore, become private, commodified property without their usefulness being crippled. But if the decisive productive force (of intelligence, knowledge) isn't susceptible of becoming a commodity, the traditional categories of political economy—labour, value and capital—are thrown into crisis.

The value of knowledge, from the standpoint of capitalist economics, is undecidable. It's impossible to measure the labour that's been expended throughout society to produce it, since knowledge is produced diffusely, wherever human beings interact, experiment, learn and dream. Knowledge isn't a homogeneous entity that can be broken down into units of production. There's no standard of measurement that can be applied to it. I take the view that it has a specific intrinsic value, different from that of commodities, comparable to that of art works, which are also not exchangeable in terms of some common yardstick. The price of knowledge has no objective basis and remains variable.

Whatever the initial cost of an item of knowledge, its exchange-value tends towards zero when it is freely accessible, can be transcribed into computer language and can be replicated indefinitely at negligible cost. In order to have an exchange-value or price, it has to be made scarce, inaccessible to everyone and privatized by a company that claims a monopoly over it and derives an income from it.

The knowledge economy is, therefore, by its very nature an economy of pooled resources and non-payment—in other words, the opposite of an economy. It spontaneously assumes this communistic form in the world of science, for example. In that world, the 'value' of an item of knowledge isn't measured in money but by the interest it evokes, by the extent of its diffusion. Underpinning the capitalist knowledge economy, we find, then, an anti-economy in which the commodity, commodity-exchange and money-making don't apply. The yardstick of wealth in that world isn't exchange-value, nor is it labour time.

This protocommunism has its emblematic figures in information technology. IT differs from science in the following specific respect: it's both knowledge, a technique for the production of knowledge, and a means of fabrication, regulation, invention and coordination. In information technology, the social division between those who produce and those who design the means of production is eliminated. The producers are no longer dominated by capital by way of the means of labour. The production of knowledge and the production of material or immaterial wealth merge. Fixed capital no longer has a separate existence; it's subsumed and internalized by men and women who concretely and practically experience that the main productive force is neither machine-capital nor money-capital, but the living passion with which they imagine and invent and increase their own cognitive capacities at the same time as their production of knowledge and wealth. Here, the production of oneself is the production of wealth and vice versa; the basis of the production of wealth is the production of oneself. Potentially, work—in the sense it has in political economy—is eliminated: 'labour . . . appears no longer as labour, but as the full development of [personal] activity itself.'[15]

The 'hacker' is the emblematic figure of this appropriation/elimination of labour. With the hacker, human productive forces, assuming subjectivity, come to rebel against their capture by capital and turn the resources of information technology around against it. It was the hacker who invented the anti-economy represented by Linux and *copyleft* (the opposite of copyright) and gave rise to the free software movement. Through the hacker, new forms of communication and regulation are appearing, together with an admirable anarcho-communist ethic—the hacker ethic—which is simultaneously an art of living, a practice of alternative individual and social relations, a pursuit of paths out of capitalism and—with that end in view—of ways to liberate our modes of thinking, feeling and desiring from its grip.

'Hackers' are not an occupational elite or an exclusive social stratum. They are part of the diffuse movement of 'digital capitalism's dissidents', to borrow Peter Glotz's expression.[16] These dissidents, who are products of the IT revolution, represent around a third of the economically active population in the United States. They include high-level programmers who reject a condition of voluntary servitude, graduates who refuse to sacrifice everything to their careers, entrepreneurs who reject that fierce competition whose watchword is 'always more, always faster', and 'jobbers' and 'downshifters' who prefer to have low incomes but plenty of time.

'The more digital capitalism extends its hold over our lives, the greater will be the number of voluntary downshifters,' writes Peter Glotz. 'A new worldview will emerge from this group. The struggle that will pit the digital proletariat against the digital elite will be over two conceptions of life based on differing principles and passions. The entire social ethos of modern capitalism is at issue.'

Notes

1 Jean-Marie Vincent (1934–2004): academic researcher
(founder and director of the Political Sciences Department of the University of Paris-VIII); editor of the
journal *Futur Antérieur*, which he co-founded with Toni
Negri; published a number of important works which
include: *Fétichisme et société* (Fetishism and Society; Paris:
Anthropos, 1973), *La Théorie critique de l'École de Francfort*
(The Critical Theory of the Frankfurt School; Paris:
Galilée, 1976), *Les Mensonges de l'État* (The Lies of the
State; Paris: Le Sycomore, 1979), *Critique du travail. Le
faire et l'agir* (Critique of Work. Making and Acting;
Paris: PUF, 1987), *Max Weber ou la démocratie inachevée*
(Max Weber or the Unfinished Democracy; Paris: Le
Félin, 1998), *Un autre Marx. Après les Marxismes* (Ano-
ther Marx. After Marxisms; Paris: Page Deux, 2001).

2 Written between *The Communist Manifesto* (1848) and the
first volume of *Capital* (1868), Marx's *Grundrisse der Kri-
tik der politischen Oekonomie* [1857–68; *Grundrisse. Foundations of the Critique of Political Economy (Rough Draft)*,
Harmondsworth: Penguin, 1973] was the book in which
he developed the foundations of his critique of political economy. See www.marxists.org/archive/marx/-
works/1857/grundrisse.

3 The journal *Futur Antérieur* was founded in 1990 by Jean-Marie Vincent, Denis Berger and Toni Negri, with the aim of promoting a revival in conceptual research and creating the conditions for a strategic, critical debate. Drawing on intellectual energies from France and Italy, it favoured three lines of theoretical development: politics, sociology and philosophy. It ceased publication in 1998.

4 André Gorz, *L'Immatériel. Connaissance, valeur et capital* (The Immaterial Economy, Paris: Galilée, 2003).

5 'Hacker' is used here in the original, positive sense of the term, as employed, for example, by Pekka Himanen (see Chapter 1, note 4), not in the later sense favoured by the tabloid press, in which it is associated with criminality. [Trans.]

6 Oekonux, a contraction of *Ökonomie* (the German for economy/economics) and Linux, studies ways of extending the principles of free software to the economy.

7 Alain Touraine, *Critique of Modernity* (Oxford: Blackwell, 1995), p. 275. [Trans.]

8 *Retooling Society* (1973) was a publication of the Centro intercultural di documentation. *Tools for Conviviality* was published by Marion Boyars of London in August 1974. [Trans.]

9 *Écologie et politique*, which was published by Éditions
   Galilée of Paris in 1975, was translated into English by
   Patsy Vigderman and Jonathan Cloud with the title *Ecol-
   ogy as Politics* (Boston: South End Press, 1980). [Trans.]

10 See Marx, *Grundrisse*, p. 702. This is explained in the
   magisterial work by the historian Moishe Postone, *Time,
   Labour and Social Domination* (Cambridge: Cambridge
   University Press, 1993), p. 363.

11 It was the subtitle of the French original. The English
   translation by Michael Sonenscher, *Farewell to the Working Class* (London: Pluto Press, 1982), bore the subtitle
   'An Essay on Post-Industrial Socialism'. [Trans.]

12 Original title: *Misères du présent: richesse du possible*. Translated by Chris Turner, in close collaboration with the
   author, the English version was published by Polity
   Press in 1999. [Trans.]

13 See note 4.

14 The reference is to the international congress staged by
   the Heinrich-Böll-Stiftung, bearing the title 'Gut zu
   Wissen. Links zur Wissensgesellschaft' [Good to Know.
   Left to the Knowledge Society] that took place in Berlin
   from 4 to 6 May 2001. [Trans.]

15 Marx, *Grundrisse*, p. 325.

16 Peter Glotz, Editor of the Germal Social Democratic Party's theoretical journal, was the author of many works, including *Der Wissenarbeiter* (The Knowledge Worker) and *Die beschleunigte Gesellschaft* (The Accelerated Society). A former Rector of the University of Erfurt and Director of the Institute for Media Research at the University of Sankt Gallen, he died in Autumn 2005.

CHAPTER ONE

THE EXIT FROM CAPITALISM HAS ALREADY BEGUN

The question of the exit from capitalism has never been more pressing. It is posed today in a radically new way and with unprecedented urgency. By its very development, capitalism has reached a limit, both internal and external, which it is incapable of transcending. It is, as a result, a system surviving the crisis of its basic categories—labour, value and capital— only by subterfuge.

The crisis of the system can be seen at both the macroeconomic and microeconomic levels. It is mainly to be explained by a techno-scientific upheaval that has produced a rupture in the development of capitalism and is, in its repercussions, destroying the basis of its power and its capacity to reproduce itself. I shall attempt to analyse this crisis from the macro-economic angle first (in section 1, below), then in its effects on the operation and management of enterprises (section 2).

1.

Computerization and automation have made it possible to produce increasing quantities of commodities with decreasing quantities of labour. The cost of labour per unit of output is constantly diminishing and the price of products is also tending to fall. The more the quantity of labour for a given output decreases, the more the value produced per worker—productivity—has to increase if the amount of achievable profit is not to fall. We have, then, this apparent paradox: the more productivity rises, the more it has to go on rising, in order to prevent the volume of profit from diminishing. Hence, the pursuit of productivity gains moves ever faster, manpower levels tend to reduce, while pressure on workers intensifies and wage levels fall, as does the overall payroll. The system is approaching an internal limit at which production and investment in production cease to be sufficiently profitable.

In China, the Philippines and Sudan, the figures show that this limit has been reached. The productive accumulation of productive capital is in constant regression. In the United States, the 500 companies listed on the Standard and Poor's Index have 631 billion dollars in liquid reserves; half the profits of American companies derive from operations in the financial markets. In France, the productive investment of the CAC40 companies is not increasing, even as their profits are rocketing.

Since production is no longer able to valorize the full amount of the accumulated capital, an increasing part of that capital remains in the form of finance capital. This leads to the formation of a *finance industry* that is constantly refining the art of making money by buying and selling nothing but various forms of money. Money itself is the only commodity the financial industry produces—through operations on the financial market that are more and more risky and less and less controllable. The amount of capital the finance industry siphons off and manages far exceeds the amount of capital valorized in the real economy (the total of financial assets represents 160 trillion dollars, which is three to four times global GDP). The 'value' of this capital is entirely fictitious: it is based largely on debt and goodwill or, in other words, on expectations. The Stock Exchange turns future growth, future company profits and future property price-rises into capital, together with the gains to be made from restructurings, mergers, amalgamations, etc. Stock market prices inflate with capital and its future profits, and households are encouraged by the banks to acquire (among other things) shares and property investments—further boosting the stock-market boom—and to borrow increasing sums from their banks, as their fictional stock-market capital grows.

The capitalization of expectations of profit and growth sustains the growing level of debt, fuels the economy with liquid assets that are the product of the banks recycling fictional profits, and enables the United States to achieve an 'economic growth' which, though based on internal and external debt, is by far the main engine of global (including Chinese) growth. The real economy is becoming an appendage of the speculative bubbles sustained by the finance industry—until that inevitable point when the bubbles burst, leading to serial bank crashes and threatening the global system of credit with collapse and the real economy with a severe, prolonged depression (the Japanese depression has been going on for almost 15 years now).

There is no point blaming speculation, tax havens, a lack of transparency in—or controls on—the finance industry, and in particular, the hedge funds. The threat of depression, if not indeed of collapse, hovering over the world economy, is not due to a lack of oversight; it is due to capitalism's incapacity to reproduce itself. It is managing to operate and perpetuate itself only on increasingly precarious fictional foundations. To seek to redistribute the fictitious profits of the speculative bubbles through taxation would bring about precisely the thing the finance industry is attempting to avoid: the devaluation of gigantic quantities of financial assets and the failure of the banking system.

'Ecological restructuring' can only aggravate the crisis of the system. It is impossible to avoid climate catastrophe without a radical break with the economic logic and methods that have been taking us in that direction for 150 years. On current trend projections, global GDP will increase by a factor of three or four by 2050. But, according to a report by the UN Climate Council, CO_2 emissions will have to fall by 85 per cent by that date to limit global warming to a maximum of 2°C . Beyond 2°C, the consequences will be irreversible and uncontrollable.

De-growth is, therefore, imperative for our survival. But it presupposes a different economy, a different lifestyle, a different civilization and different social relations. In the absence of these, collapse could be avoided only through restrictions, rationing and the kind of authoritarian resource-allocation typical of a *war economy. The exit from capitalism will happen, then, one way or another,* in either a civilized or barbarous fashion. The question is simply what form it will take and how quickly it will occur.

We are already familiar with the barbarous form. It prevails in several regions of Africa, which are dominated by warlords, by the pillaging of the wreckage of modernity, by massacres and by the trafficking of human beings, the whole taking place against a background of famine. The three *Mad Max* films represented the 'shape of things to come'.

Only very rarely, by contrast, is a civilized exit from capitalism envisaged. Mention of looming climate catastrophe generally leads to envisaging a necessary 'change of mindset', but the nature of that change, its conditions of possibility and the obstacles to be overcome seem to defy all imagining. To envisage a different economy, different social relations, different modes and means of production and different ways of life is regarded as 'unrealistic', as though the society based on commodities, wages and money could not be surpassed. In reality, a whole host of convergent indices suggest that *the surpassing of that society is already under way*, and that the chances of a civilized exit from capitalism depend primarily on our capacity to discern the trends and practices that herald its possibility.

2.

Capitalism owes its expansion and domination to the power it has assumed, within the space of a century, over both production and consumption. By first dispossessing the workers of their means of labour and of their products, it gradually acquired the monopoly of the means of production and the ability to subsume labour. By specializing, dividing and mechanizing work in large industrial plants, it turned the workers into appendages of the megamachines of capital. Any appropriation of the means of production by the producers became impossible as a result. By eliminating the producers' power over nature and the destination of their production, it gave capital a virtual monopoly of supply, and hence the power to promote the most profitable production and consumption in all fields, as well as the power to shape the tastes and desires of consumers and the way they would satisfy their needs. It is this power the IT revolution is beginning to fissure.

It was, initially, the goal of computerization to reduce production costs. To avoid this cost-reduction leading to a corresponding fall in the prices of commodities, those commodities had, as far as possible, to be withdrawn from the laws of the market. This withdrawal consisted in conferring *incomparable qualities* on commodities, by virtue of which they seemed to have *no equivalent*, and hence not to appear as mere commodities.

The commercial value (price) of the products was, then, to depend more on their non-measurable *immaterial qualities* than on their substantial utility (use-value). These immaterial qualities—style, novelty, brand prestige, scarcity or 'exclusiveness'—were to confer on products a status comparable to that of art works. These latter have an intrinsic value; there is no scale by which a *relation of equivalence* or 'true price' can be established between them. They are not, therefore, real commodities. Their price depends on their scarcity, on the reputation of the artist who made them and the desire of the potential buyer. The incomparable immaterial qualities procure for the producing firm the equivalent of a monopoly and the possibility of deriving a *rent* from novelty, scarcity or exclusivity. This rent conceals and compensates (and often over-compensates) for the fall in value in the economic sense that the lowering of production costs entails for the products as commodities which are, in their essence, exchangeable one for another, given the relation of equivalence between them. From the economic standpoint, then, innovation does not create value: it is the way to create scarcity, a source of rent, and to obtain a price supplement, to the detriment of rival products. The proportion of the price of a commodity that is rent may be 10, 20 or 50 times larger than its production cost. And this is true not only of luxury items; it applies also to everyday articles like trainers, T-shirts, mobile phones, CDs, jeans, etc.

Now, rent is not like profit: it does not correspond to the creation of an additional quantum of value, a surplus-value. It *redistributes* the total amount of value towards the *rentier* enterprises and away from the others, but it does not increase that amount.[1]

When it becomes the key goal of companies' policies to increase rents—when rent becomes more important than profit which, for its part, runs up against the internal limit mentioned above—competition between companies comes to be about their capacity for, and their speed of, innovation. This is what the size of their rents mainly depends on. As a result, they try to outdo each other in launching new products, models or styles, to excel in the originality of their design, the inventiveness of their marketing campaigns or the 'personalization' of their products. The acceleration of obsolescence, which goes hand in hand with reducing product durability and reparability, becomes the crucial way of boosting sales figures. It forces firms to invent new needs and desires constantly, to confer a symbolic, social, erotic value on commodities, to spread a 'consumer culture' predicated on individualization, singularization, rivalry and jealousy—in a word, on what I have elsewhere termed 'anti-social socialization'.

Everything in that system stands opposed to the autonomy of individuals, to their capacity to reflect together on their common ends and shared needs, to agree on the best way of eliminating waste, to conserve resources and to develop together, as producers and consumers, a common norm of 'the sufficient'— or of what Jacques Delors has called a 'frugal abundance'. Quite clearly, breaking with the 'produce more, consume more' trend and redefining a model of life aimed at *doing more and better with less* presupposes breaking with a civilization in which we produce nothing of what we consume and consume nothing of what we produce; in which producers and consumers are separated, and in which everyone is opposed to herself inasmuch as she is always both producer and consumer at the same time; in which all needs and all desires lead back to the need to earn money and the desire to earn more; in which the possibility of producing for one's own consumption seems—wrongly—out of reach and ridiculously archaic.

And yet 'the dictatorship over needs' is losing its power. Despite the explosion of expenditure on marketing and advertising, the hold that corporations have over consumers is becoming more fragile. The trend towards self-providing is gaining ground again as a result of the increasing proportion of immaterial contents in the nature of commodities. The monopoly on supply is gradually slipping away from capital.

It was not difficult to privatize and monopolize immaterial contents so long as the knowledge, ideas and concepts deployed in the production and design of commodities were defined as a function of machines and of articles in which they were incorporated with a view to a precise usage. The machines and articles could be patented and the monopoly position protected. Private ownership of knowledge and concepts was made possible by the fact that they were inseparable from the objects that embodied them materially. They were components of fixed capital.

But everything changes when the immaterial contents are no longer inseparable from the products that contain them, nor even from the persons in possession of them; when they acquire an existence independent of any particular use and are capable, once translated into software, of being reproduced in unlimited quantities at negligible cost. They can then become a plentiful good which, by its unlimited availability, loses all exchange-value and falls into the public domain as *free common property*, unless it is successfully prevented from doing so by forbidding accesss to it and to the unlimited use to which it lends itself.

The problem the 'knowledge economy' runs up against arises from the fact that, in the age of information technology, the immaterial dimension on which the profitability of commodities depends is not of the same nature as those commodities: it is neither the *private property* of corporations nor of their collaborators; by its very nature, it is not privatizable and cannot, as a consequence, become a genuine commodity. It can be *disguised* as private property and as a commodity only by reserving the exclusive use of it through legal or technical artifices (secret access codes). But this disguise changes nothing about the reality of the good so disguised, which is a reality of common property: it remains a non-saleable non-commodity, free access to which and free use of which are forbidden, *because such access and use always remain possible*, because 'illegal copies', 'imitations' and forbidden uses are always a threat. The so-called owners themselves cannot sell these goods—that is to say, transfer the private ownership of them to someone else—as they would with a genuine commodity; they can sell only a right of access or a right of use 'under licence'.

Thus, the knowledge economy depends on a form of wealth that tends naturally towards the status of common property, and the patents and copyrights that are supposed to privatize that common property make no difference to this: the sphere of what is free is spreading irresistibly. Information technology and the Internet are undermining the reign of commodities at its foundations. Everything translatable into digital language and reproducible or communicable at no cost tends irresistibly to become common property, if not indeed universal common property, when it is accessible to—and useable by—everyone. Using a computer, anyone can reproduce such immaterial contents as designs, building or assembly plans, chemical formulae and equations; anyone can invent their own styles and forms, print texts, burn disks, reproduce pictures. More than 200 million items are currently accessible under 'creative commons' licences.

In Brazil, where the music industry brings out 15 new CDs a year, the young people of the *favelas* burn twenty-four *per week* and distribute them on the streets. Three-quarters of the computers produced in 2004 were self-produced in the *favelas* from cast-off components. The government supports cooperatives and informal self-providing groups. Claudio Prado, Director of the Department of Digital Culture within the Brazilian Culture Ministry, said recently: 'Employment is an endangered species . . . We are reckoning on bypassing the bullshit of the twentieth century' and . . . 'jumping from the nineteenth century to the twenty-first'. The self-production of computers has, for example, received official support: the aim is to promote 'the appropriation of technologies by the users for purposes of social transformation.' Logically, the next stage will be the self-production of means of production. I shall come back to this.

The important point for now is that the main productive force and the main source of rents are gradually falling into the public domain and tending to become cost-free; the private ownership of the means of production, and hence monopoly supply, are gradually becoming impossible; and as a consequence, capital's grip on consumption is being loosened and consumption is tending to become emancipated from commodity supply. This is a revolution that is undermining capitalism at its base. The battle between 'proprietary software' and freeware represents the opening salvo in the central conflict of the age. That conflict continues and widens in the struggle against the commodification of the primary forms of wealth—the earth, seeds, the genome, cultural goods and the shared knowledge and skills that make up the culture of everyday life and are the preconditions for the existence of a society. Whether the exit from capitalism assumes a civilized or barbarous form depends on the way this struggle turns out.

That exit necessarily implies that we free ourselves from the grip capital has exerted on consumption and from its monopoly of the means of production. It means re-establishing the unity between the subject of production and the subject of consumption, and hence recovering autonomy in the definition of our needs and their mode of satisfaction. The insurmountable obstacle capitalism laid across this path was the actual nature of the means of production it established: these constituted a megamachine that everyone was made to serve and that dictated to us the ends we were to pursue and the lives we were to live. That period is coming to an end. High-tech self-providing equipment is rendering the industrial megamachine virtually obsolete. Claudio Prado speaks of the 'appropriation of technologies', because the key that is common to all of them—information technology—can be appropriated by everyone; because, as Illich demanded, 'everyone can use it without difficulty, as often as he or she likes . . . without the use he or she makes of it infringing the freedom of others to do likewise'; and because that use (this is Illich's definition of convivial tools) boosts 'personal fulfilment' and increases everyone's autonomy. The definition Pekka Himanen gives of the 'hacker ethic' is very similar to this: a mode of life that puts the joys of friendship, love, free cooperation and personal creativity first.[2]

Existing tools or tools currently in development, which are generally comparable to computer peripherals, point towards a future in which it will be possible to produce practically all that is necessary and desirable in cooperative or communal workshops; in which it will be possible to combine productive activities with learning and teaching, with experimentation and research, with the creation of new tastes, flavours and materials, and with the invention of new forms and techniques of agriculture, building and medicine, etc. Communal self-providing workshops will be globally interconnected, will be able to exchange or share their experiences, inventions, ideas and discoveries. Work will be a producer of culture, and self-providing will be a way to self-fulfilment.

Two things argue for a development of this type. First, many more skills and talents exist than the capitalist economy can use—and also much more creativity. This surplus of human resources can become productive only in an economy in which wealth creation is not subject to the criteria of profitability. The second is that 'employment is an endangered species.'

I do not say that these radical transformations will come about. I am simply saying that, for the first time, we can wish them to come about. The means exist, as well as the people who are methodically working towards their realization. It will probably be South Americans or South Africans who are the first to re-create, in the deprived suburbs of Europe's cities, the self-providing workshops of their native *favelas* or *townships*.

Notes

1 'Labour value' is an idea of Adam Smith. Labour was for him the common substance in all commodities and he believed that commodities traded at a price proportional to the quantity of labour they contained. Marx

refined and reworked Smith's theory. Simplifying greatly, we may sum up the *economic* notion of value by saying that an enterprise *creates value* insofar as it produces a saleable commodity with labour which it remunerates by putting in circulation (creating or distributing) a quantity of purchasing power. If its activity does not increase the quantity of money in circulation, it does not create value. If its activity destroys employment, it destroys value. Monopoly rents consume value created elsewhere and appropriate it for themselves. Personal services do not create value, but redistribute it.

2 See Pekka Himanen, *The Hacker Ethic and the Spirit of the Information Age* (London: Secker and Warburg, 2001), especially pp. 3–6.

CHAPTER TWO

POLITICAL ECOLOGY

BETWEEN EXPERTOCRACY AND SELF-LIMITATION

For Dick Howard

Depending on whether it is scientific or political, ecology covers two distinct but interconnected approaches. I shall begin by stressing the difference rather than the interconnectedness of their objects, since it is important to avoid the political approach being presented as the option that must be adopted as an 'absolute necessity' in the light of 'scientific analysis'. That would merely reproduce in a new form the kind of anti-political, scientistic dogmatism which, in its 'Diamat' version, claimed to raise political practices and conceptions to the rank of manifest scientific necessities, thereby denying their specifically political character.

As a science, ecology shows civilization in its interaction with the terrestrial ecosystem or, in other words, with what forms the natural basis or non-(re)producible context of human activity. Unlike industrial systems, the natural ecosystem has a capacity for self-generation and self-organization which, thanks to its extreme diversity and complexity, enables it to regulate itself and evolve in the direction of increasing complexity and diversity. This capacity for self-regeneration and self-reorganization is damaged by technologies that tend to rationalize and dominate nature, to make it predictable and calculable. 'Our technological surges,' writes Edgar Morin, 'disturb not only biological cycles, but primary chemical loops. In response, we develop control technologies which highlight the effects of these ills while amplifying their causes.'[1]

EXPERTOCRACY

Given this situation, two approaches are possible. The first, based on the scientific study of the ecosystem, seeks to determine scientifically which technologies and what pollution thresholds are ecologically tolerable—in other words, the conditions and limits within which the development of the industrial technosphere can be pursued without compromising the self-generative capacities of the ecosphere. This approach does not break fundamentally with industrialism and its hegemony of instrumental reason. It recognizes the need to limit the ransacking of natural resources and replace it with a long-term, rational management of air, water, soils, forests and oceans, which involves policies of waste reduction, recycling and the development of environmentally non-destructive technologies.

Hence, unlike political ecology, policies of environmental conservation in no sense tend towards a pacification of the relations with nature or 'reconciliation' with it; they tend to 'manage' it (in the dual sense of commanding it and coping with it), while taking account of the *necessity* of at least preserving its most basic capacities for self-regeneration. From this necessity, measures will be deduced that have to be implemented in the interests of humanity as a whole and that states have to force economic decision-makers and individual consumers to respect.

In this case, the consideration of ecological constraints by states will take the form of prohibitions, administrative regulations, taxation, subsidies and penalties. The effect will consequently be to reinforce the *hetero-regulation* of society's functioning. This will have to become more or less 'eco-compatible', *irrespective of the personal intentions* of the social actors. 'Regulative media', such as administrative authority and the price system, are allotted the task of channelling consumer behaviour and investor decisions towards a goal that can be achieved without their needing to either approve or understand it. They will achieve it because the administration will have managed to functionalize individual interests and motivations to attain an outcome that remains foreign to them. According to its advocates, fiscal and monetary hetero-regulation has the advantage of leading to the goal of eco-compatibility without any need for a change in the mentalities, value system or economic interests and motivations of the social actors. On the contrary, it is by basing itself on these motivations and interests, *while at the same time manipulating them*, that the goal is achieved. Pursuing it thus involves an extension of what Habermas called 'the colonization of the life-world'—in other words, the use by the system managers of existing individual motivations, to make them produce outcomes that do not correspond to any intentions on the part of the individuals.

The consideration of ecological constraints thus finds expression, within the framework of industrialism and market logic, in an extension of techno-bureaucratic power. But this approach is the product of a typically anti-political, pre-modern conception. It abolishes the autonomy of the political, replacing it with expertocracy, by making the state and state experts judges of what constitutes the general interest and of the means of *subordinating* individuals to it. The universal is separated from the particular, and the higher interest of humanity from freedom and from individuals' autonomous capacity for judgement. Now, as Dick Howard has shown,[2] politics is defined initially by its bipolar structure: it has to be—and can only be—the ever-renewed public mediation between the rights of individuals, based on their autonomy, and the interests of society as a whole, which both founds and conditions those rights. Any approach tending to abolish the tension between these two poles is a negation of both politics and modernity. And, of course, this goes particularly for the expertocracies, which deny individuals the capacity to judge and subject them to an 'enlightened' power that speaks in the name of the higher interest of a cause beyond their understanding.

Herein lies the source of the ambiguity of the ecological imperative: as soon as it is taken on board by the various power apparatuses, it serves to reinforce their domination over daily life and the social environment and comes into conflict with the original aspirations of the ecological movement itself as a politico-cultural movement. This is the underlying reason for the internal split within that movement between a technocratic and a radical-democratic wing.

THE ORIGINAL SENSE OF THE MOVEMENT

The ecological movement formed long before environmental degradation and the impairment of the quality of life came to pose a threat to humanity's survival. It arose originally out of a spontaneous protest against the destruction of the *culture of daily life* by the economic and administrative apparatuses of power. And by 'culture of everyday life', I mean the entire range of forms of intuitive knowledge, of vernacular skills (in Illich's sense of the term), of habits, norms and commonplace behaviour through which individuals can interpret, understand and come to terms with how they fit into the world around them.

The 'nature' which the movement demanded should be protected was neither the Nature of the naturalists, nor that of scientific ecology: it was, basically, the milieu that seems 'natural' because its structures and its operation are accessible to an intuitive understanding; because it matches the need for our sensory and motor faculties to thrive; because its familiar conformation enables individuals to orient themselves within it, interact, and communicate 'spontaneously' by virtue of aptitudes that have never had to be formally taught.

The 'defence of nature' must be understood, then, originally as the defence of a *lifeworld*, which is defined, among other things, by the fact that the outcome of activities corresponds to the intentions behind those activities—in other words, by the fact that, in that world, social individuals see, understand and control the outcomes of their acts.

The more complex a society becomes, the less intuitively intelligible is its operation. The mass of knowledge deployed in production, administration, trade and law far exceeds the capacities of an individual or group. Each of these has only a partial, specialized knowledge, which pre-established organizational procedures—apparatuses—will coordinate and organize to achieve an outcome that lies beyond what individuals are capable of wishing for. In this way, complex societies are like enormous machineries: insofar as they are social, they are *systems* whose operation demands individuals who are *functionally specialized*, like the organs of a body or the components of a machine. However complex and sophisticated they may be, forms of knowledge that have become specialized to meet the systematic demands of the social totality no longer contain sufficient cultural resources to enable individuals to orient themselves in the world, to endow what they are doing with meaning or to understand the sense of what they are working towards. The system invades and marginalizes the lifeworld, in the sense of the world accessible to intuitive understanding and practico-sensorial apprehension. It deprives individuals of the possibility of having—and sharing—a world. It is against the various forms of this expropriation that resistance was gradually organized.

The first actions of what was to become the eco-logical movement were directed—first in North America, then in Europe—against the megatech-nologies in favour of which private industries and/or public administrations deprived the citizens of their human environment.[3] That environment was revolu-tionized, technicized, concreted over and colonized to meet the demands of the industrial megamachine. This megamachine took from the inhabitants the little that remained to them of a 'natural' environment, sub-jected them to nuisance and pollution, and, more fun-damentally, confiscated the public domain for technical apparatuses that symbolized *the violation by capital and the state of the right of individuals* themselves to determine their way of living together, producing and consuming.

This violation was particularly flagrant in the case of atomic power: the nuclear building programme depended on politico-economic decisions dressed up as technically rational, socially necessary options. It forecast a very high increase in energy needs, gave preference to the highest concentration of the heaviest technologies to meet those needs, and created bodies of technicians sworn to professional secrecy and subject to quasi-military discipline. In short, it made the assessment of needs and of how those needs were to be met, the preserve of a caste of experts, sheltering behind a higher form of knowledge that was allegedly beyond the reach of the population. It posed as the guardian of that population in the interests of the most capital-intensive industries and reinforced domination by the state apparatus.[4] The same kind of authority over the population operates more diffusely in all those fields where professionalization—and the legal formalization and the specialization it entails—discredits vernacular knowledge and destroys individuals' capacity to take charge of their own lives. These are the 'disabling professions' denounced by Illich.[5]

Resistance to this destruction of the capacity to take charge of one's own life—in other words, of the existential autonomy of individuals and groups or communities—lies at the origin of certain specific components of the ecological movement: patient self-help networks, movements for alternative therapies, the campaign for abortion rights, the campaign for the right to die 'in dignity', movements for the defence of languages, cultures and regions, etc. The deep motivation is always to defend the 'lifeworld' against the rule of experts, against monetary evaluation and quantification and against substituting commodity and clientelist relations and relations of dependency for the autonomy and self-determination of individuals.

In appearance at least, the movement was purely 'cultural'. Insofar as the political parties were preoccupied, above all, with the power to *manage the system* in the interest of their electoral *clienteles*, the ecological movement necessarily seemed to them anti-political: it was concerned with 'changing life', with freeing life from the system and those who ran it, by attempting to win back spaces of lived autonomy and sociality from that system.

After 1972, these seemingly cultural demands were put on an objective footing by a report produced by a group of British scientists, *Blueprint for Survival*, and shortly afterwards by the report commissioned by the Club of Rome entitled *Limits to Growth*. The impossibility of carrying on down the industrial economies' path of growth, the destructiveness of the capitalist model of development and consumption, and the severing of the link between 'more' and 'better' necessitated a radical change in the techniques and goals of production, and hence a radical change in lifestyles. In this way, the 'cultural' demands of the ecological movement found themselves objectively underpinned by the urgent, scientifically demonstrable need to break with the dominant industrialism and its religion of growth. Environmentalism *could*, therefore, become a political movement, since the defence of the lifeworld was not merely a sectoral and local aspiration lacking in general scope, but was shown to be consonant with the general interest of humanity and of the living world as a whole.

However, the converse is not true. As we have seen, concern for the ecological interests of humanity does not *necessarily* assume the form (desirable from the standpoint of individuals) of a defence—or, more exactly, reconquest—of the lifeworld. It may, indeed, take the technocratic form of greater constraint and manipulation by the administrative subsystem. It is impossible to base politics on a necessity or a science without thereby denying it in its specific autonomy and establishing a 'necessary', 'scientific' dictatorship which is just as totalitarian when it appeals to the demands of the ecosystem as when it appeals (like the philosophy of 'Diamat') to the 'laws of dialectical materialism'.

Hence, the problem facing political ecology is the problem of the practical ways in which the demands of the ecosystem can be taken into account in autonomous individuals' own judgements, as they pursue their own ends within their lifeworlds. It is the problem of the retroactive coupling between necessity and normativity or, to put it another way, of the translation of objective necessities into normative behaviours corresponding to lived demands, in the light of which the objective necessities are shaped in their turn. This is, quite simply, the problem of democracy.

SELF-LIMITATION

To Marx, this problem seemed soluble insofar as industrialism was to generate the objective conditions and subjective capacity for generalized self-management. It was to lead to a (Communist) society in which

> [. . .] socialized man, the associated produc-
> ers, govern the human metabolism with na-
> ture in a rational way, bringing it under their
> collective control instead of being domi-
> nated by it as a blind power; accomplishing it
> with the least expenditure of energy and in
> conditions most worthy and appropriate for
> their human nature. But this always remains
> a realm of necessity. The true realm of free-

dom [. . .] can only flourish with this realm of necessity as its basis.[6]

In other words, necessity is accepted by the associated producers as part of a twofold normative exigency: on the one hand, to gain the highest satisfaction in their work for the least expenditure of effort and, on the other, to manage 'the human metabolism with nature' in a rational, universally intelligible way. The rationality of that management will consist in both attending to the ecosystem and employing means of production which the associated producers can control, that is to say, which they can manage for themselves instead of being dominated by their giganticism and complexity.

Within the framework of worker self-management, freedom will depend on the ability of the 'associated producers' to *decide* between the quantity and quality of work that different means and methods of production require per unit of output, and *between the extent of the needs and desires they wish to satisfy and the amount of effort they are willing to deploy*. This decision, based on lived, shared norms will lead, for example, to working in a more relaxed and gratifying way ('most appropriate for their human nature'), at the expense of a lower level of productivity. It will lead also to *limiting needs and desires, so as to be able to limit the effort that has to be expended.* In practice, the norm by which the level of effort is set as a function of the level of satisfaction sought—and, conversely, the level of satisfaction as a function of the effort one is prepared to put in—is the norm of *sufficiency.*

Now, establishing a norm of sufficiency is incompatible, given the self-limitation of needs and effort that it implies, with the pursuit of maximum output that constitutes the essence of economic rationality and rationalization. Economic rationality was never, in fact, able to express itself in its essential nature in precapitalist societies. It was always 'embedded' in those societies, as Karl Polanyi puts it, that is to say, hemmed and hedged about by agreements between producers and merchants to prohibit free competition in free markets. It never proved possible to impose it on pro-

ducers, so long as they controlled their means of production and were, as a consequence, free to determine
for themselves the intensity, duration and scheduling
of their work. The decline in production for one's own
use and the expansion of production for the market
changed nothing of this: the corporations or guilds dictated to the merchants uniform prices for each quality
of product defined by them and strictly prohibited any
form of competition. The relations between producers and merchants were solidly contractual and it suited
the merchants themselves to be sheltered from free-
market competition. The norm of *sufficiency*—sufficient
earnings for the artisan, sufficient profit for the mer-
chant—was so deeply rooted in the traditional mode
of life that it was impossible to get more intense or
longer labour from workers by offering them higher
earnings. The worker 'did not ask,' writes Max Weber,
'how much can I earn in a day if I do as much work as
possible? But: how much must I work in order to earn
the wage, two and a half marks, which I earned before
and which takes care of my traditional needs?'[7]

In *Volume One* of *Capital*, Marx cites a vast range of sources that attest to the extreme difficulty experienced by the owners of the manufactories and the first 'automatic factories' in obtaining regular, full-time work from their labour force day after day and week after week. To force them to perform such work, it was not enough to take the *ownership* of the means of production from them, as the factory owners had done. After first ruining the craft producers, it was also necessary to reduce the pay of workers per unit of output in order to force them to work more to obtain a *sufficiency*. And to this end, *control* of the means of production had to be taken from them, so that a form of work organization and division of labour could be imposed in which the nature, quantity and intensity of the work to be performed would be dictated to them as constraints built into their material situation.

Mechanization provided the optimum means for achieving this result. For the means of production driven and handled by workers, it substituted machines set in motion by an automaton, a moving power that moves itself [. . .] In no way does the machine appear as the individual worker's means of labour [. . .] The worker's activity, reduced to a mere abstraction of activity, is determined and regulated on all sides by the movement of the machinery [. . .] The science which compels the inanimate limbs of the machinery, by their construction, to act purposefully, as an automaton, does not exist in the worker's consciousness, but rather acts upon him through the machine as an alien power, as the power of the machine itself. The appropriation of living labour by objectified labour, [. . .] which lies in the concept of capital, is posited, in production resting on machinery, as the character of the production process itself.[8]

The individual worker is now 'a mere living accessory of this machinery'; his 'individual labour capacity is an infinitesimal, vanishing magnitude; the production in enormous mass quantities which is posited with machinery destroys every connection of the product with the direct need of the producer, and hence with direct use-value."[9]

It could not be more clearly stated that the instrument of labour is thus rendered *inappropriable* by the workers and that both this separation of producers and product, and the separation of the workers from work itself—which now exists as something external to them, as the silent exigency built into the material organization of production, for quantified, predetermined, strictly programmed tasks—need to be effected.[10]

It is only on the basis of this triple dispossession that production can free itself from the decisional power of the direct producers or, in other words, become independent of the relation between the needs and desires they feel, the exent of the effort they are prepared to expend to satisfy those needs and desires, and the intensity, duration and quality of that effort.

It is also this triple dispossession that made possible increasingly narrow functional specializations and the accumulation and combination, in a single production process, of a mass of techno-scientific knowledge from heterogeneous disciplines, which were incapable of communicating with each other and were resistant to coordination, and hence required a general staff and a quasi-military pyramidal structure if they were to be organized for productive ends.

It was only on this basis that industrialization or, in other words, the accumulation of capital, was possible. It was only by separating the direct producers from the means and output of production that it was possible to make them produce surpluses exceeding their needs and to use those 'economic surpluses' to increase the quantity and potency of the means of production. Supposing the means of production had been developed originally by the associated producers themselves, enterprises would have remained controllable by them; they would have carried on self-limiting *both* their needs *and* the nature and inten-

sity of their labour. As a consequence, industrialization would not have led to concentrations which, by
their scale and complexity, lie beyond the decisional
power of the producers. 'Economic development'
could not have gone beyond a certain threshold; competition would have been contained; and the norm of
sufficiency would have continued to govern 'the
human metabolism with nature'.

By eliminating the power of the direct producers
in and over production, capital was ultimately able to
emancipate production from felt needs and to select
or create needs, together with ways of meeting them,
on the basis of what would achieve the greatest profitability. Production thus became, first and foremost,
a *way* for capital to increase; it is, primarily, in the service of capital's 'needs', and it is only insofar as capital
needs consumers for its products that production also
serves human needs. However, these are no longer
'natural' needs or desires, spontaneously felt. They are
needs and desires *produced* to meet the needs of capital's return on its investment. The needs that capital

serves are used by it for its own growth. And, if it is to grow, that growth in turn requires needs. Developed capitalism's model of consumption is, thus, the product of the demand inherent in capital that it create the greatest possible number of needs and satisfy those needs with the greatest possible flow of commodities. Pursuit of maximum efficiency in valorizing capital thus requires maximum inefficiency in meeting needs. It requires maximum wastage.

This process whereby production became an autonomous process would have been much more difficult if the workers could have tailored the length of their working day to the income they felt they needed. As productivity and wages rose, an increasing fraction of the working population would have—or could have—chosen to work less and self-limit the growth of their consumption. This trend did, in fact, reaffirm itself at the height of the anarcho-syndicalist movement in the form of the intermittent working or the three- or four-day weeks worked, among other places, in the Paris iron and steel plants, by the *sublimes simples* and *vrais sublimes* of whom Denis Poulot writes.[11] Against this reappearance of a self-limitation in terms of the norm of sufficiency, a strict regulation of employment conditions was introduced in Britain in 1910, restricting recruitment to those committed to full-time working. By making full-time work the condition of employment, capital not only ensured its domination of the workforce and the predictability of output and of labour costs, it also extended its domination over the workers' way of life. It left room in their lives only for functional, paid work in the service of capital, on the one hand, and consumption in the service of capital, on the other. Social individuals were to define themselves as worker-consumers, as 'clients' of capital, insofar as they depended both on wages received and on commodities bought. They were to produce nothing of what they consumed and consume nothing of what they produced. They were to have no public, social existence outside the existence mediated by capital: non-working time was to remain the time of *private* existence, entertainment, rest and 'holidaying'. The demand to reduce working hours has always been the one the employers have fought most bitterly. They have preferred to grant longer paid holidays, since holidays are, above all else, a programmed *interruption* of working life, a time of pure consumption that does not form part of every-day life, enhance it with new dimensions, confer in-creased autonomy on it or give it a content other than the narrowly occupational.

SELF-LIMITATION AS A SOCIAL PROJECT

In complex industrial societies, it is impossible to achieve an eco-compatible restructuring of produc-tion and consumption merely by giving the workers the right to self-limit their work or, in other words, by giving them the option of choosing their working hours. No *obvious correlation* exists, in fact, between vol-ume of production and working hours. Since au-tomation has abolished this correlation by making it possible to produce more and more wealth with less and less labour, 'as soon as labour in the direct form has ceased to be the great well-spring of wealth, labour time ceases . . . to be its measure.'[12] Moreover, decreasing the volume of necessary labour brings no benefit to the whole of the potentially active population; it brings neither emancipation nor a hope of greater autonomy either to those in work or to the unemployed. Ultimately, there is no commonly accepted norm of 'sufficiency' that could serve as a reference for self-limitation. And yet, self-limitation remains the only non-authoritarian, democratic path towards an eco-compatible industrial civilization.

However, the difficulty we have run up against here is in no way insurmountable. It means, essentially, that capitalism has abolished everything in tradition, our way of life and daily civilization that could serve as an anchoring point for a common norm of sufficiency, and that it has, at the same time, abolished the view that the decision to work and consume less can give access to a better, freer life. However, what has been abolished can conceivably be restored. But that restoration cannot be based on a tradition or on existing correlations: it has to be established from scratch; it is of a political or, more precisely, eco-political order, and relates to the eco-social project.

The fundamental point of an eco-social politics, as debated over a long period by the German and European Greens during the 1980s[13] and as it is emerging today in French political ecology,[14] is to *re-establish politically the correlation between less work and consumption, on the one hand, and more existential autonomy and security for all, on the other.* In other words, it is a question of institutionally guaranteeing to individuals that a general reduction in working hours will open up for all the advantages that everyone could in the past have obtained for themselves: namely, a freer, more relaxed, more rewarding life. In this way, self-limitation has shifted from the level of individual choice to the level of the social project. Since we lack any traditional point of anchorage for it, we have to define the norm of sufficiency politically.

Without entering into detail here over questions I have discussed elsewhere, I shall simply recall that eco-social policy consists mainly in making the guarantee of a minimum income independent of the length of hours worked (which are bound to decrease) and, potentially, independent of work itself; in redistributing socially necessary labour in such a way that everyone can work, and work both better and less; in creating spaces of autonomy in which the time freed from work can be employed by individuals on activities of their own choosing, including the self-providing of goods and services that will reduce their dependency on the market and on professional or administrative provision and enable them to reconstitute a fabric of lived solidarities and sociality, made up of mutual support networks, exchanges of services and informal co-operatives. The freeing of time and the liberation from heteronomous, functionally specialized work must be conceived as a joined-up policy, and this requires that we also rethink architecture and town-planning, public facilities and services and relations between the town and the countryside in such a way as to break down barriers between different spheres of life and activity, and promote self-organized exchanges.[15]

In this way, political ecology turns those changes in our ways of producing and consuming that are ecologically *necessary* into the levers for achieving normatively *desirable* changes in our way of life and social relations. The defence of the *environment* in the ecological sense and the reconstitution of a *lifeworld* condition and support each other. Both demand that life and the environment be withdrawn from the domination of the economy, and that the spheres of activity be expanded in which economic rationality does not apply. This demand is, in truth, as old as civilization. From the anonymous Ricardian, whose 1821 pamphlet Marx liked to quote, to Keynes and Leontieff, the great theorists of the modern economy have all seen 'disposable time' for activity that is 'an end in itself' (*'die sich als Selbstzweck gilt'*, as Marx says in *Capital, Volume 3*) as 'the true measure of wealth'. That is equivalent to saying that economic activity has meaning only in the service of something else. This is because economics is, above all else, a form of 'cognitive-instrumental reason'. That is to say, it is a science for calculating the efficiency of the means—and the choice of the most efficient means—

to deploy in pursuit of an end. It is inapplicable to ends that are not distinct from the means employed, and it cannot itself determine the ends to be pursued. When no end is prescribed for it, it chooses those ends for which it possesses the most efficient means: it will take as its goal the growth of the sphere in which its rationality can be deployed and tend to subordinate all other spheres, including life and the natural foundations of life, to that one.

This domination of all other forms of rationality by economic rationality is the essence of capitalism. Left to itself, it will end in the extinction of life, and hence its own extinction. If it is to have a meaning, that meaning can only be to create the conditions for its own abolition.

Notes

1 Edgar Morin, *La Vie de la vie* (The Life of Life; Paris: Le Seuil, 1980), pp. 94–5.

2 Particularly in the preface to the second edition of *From Marx to Kant* (London: Macmillan/New York: St Mar-

tin's Press, 1992). See also the same author's excellent *The Marxian Legacy* (London: Macmillan, 1988). I gave a closely related definition of the political in the final chapter and 'Postscript' of *Farewell to the Working Class*.

3 This is clearly not the only form of protest against the destruction of the lifeworld. Chauvinism, racism, xenophobia and anti-semitism are all forms of rejection of the incomprehensible, threatening complexity of a changing world. They explain the disappearance of its familiar order in terms of a conspiracy of evil foreign forces and the corruption of the ruling classes. In other words, they explain a reality that has become inaccessible to intuitive understanding by causes which *are* intuitively accessible.

4 In *Anti-nuclear Protest: the Opposition to Nuclear Energy in France* (New York/Paris: Cambridge University Press-Éditions de la Maison des sciences de l'homme, 1983), Alain Touraine et al. showed that, in stressing the danger of the power stations, the movement was motivated not by fear, but by the desire to contest the omniscience in which the experts cloaked themselves, at the risk of diverting the debate off into technical squabbles to the detriment of its political content.

5 See *Limits to Medicine: Medical Nemesis—The Expropriation of Health* (London: Marion Boyars, 1976), *The Right*

to Useful Unemployment (London: Marion Boyars, 1978) and *Shadow Work* (London: Marion Boyars, 1981).

6 Karl Marx, *Capital, Volume 3*. Translated by David Fernbach (London: Penguin Classics, 1991), p. 959.

7 Max Weber, *The Protestant Ethic and the Spirit of Capitalism* (London: Unwin Paperbacks, 1985), p. 60.

8 Marx, *Grundrisse*, pp. 692–3.

9 Ibid., pp. 693–4.

10 I have shown elsewhere that machinery and the science given material form in it are not appropriable by the collective labourer (*Gesamtarbeiter*) either. That collective labourer encompasses a multiplicity of functionally specialized, separate and dispersed collectives, making it practically impossible for collectives to consult together and have control over the final product. That control would require an organization and management teams which, as in the combines of the former GDR, would reproduce the separation and dispossession referred to above.

11 Denis Poulot, *Le Sublime, ou le travailleur comme il est en 1870 et ce qu'il peut être* (The 'Sublime', or The Worker as he is in 1870 and what he can be; Paris: La Découverte, 1980). See also the excellent study by Christian Topalov, 'Invention du chômage et politiques sociales au début du siècle' (The Invention of Unemployment and Social

Policies at the Beginning of the Century), *Les Temps modernes*, 496–497 (November–December 1987).

12 Marx, *Grundrisse*, p. 705.

13 I shall cite only four works here that contain an extensive bibliography: Michael Opielka (ed.), *Die Ökosoziale Frage* (The Eco-Social Question; Frankfurt-am-Main: Fischer Alternativ, 1985); Joseph Huber, *Die Regenbogengesellschaft. Ökologie und Sozialpolitik* (The Rainbow Society. Ecology and Social Policy; Frankfurt-am-Main: Fischer Alternativ, 1985); Michael Opielka and Georg Vobruba (eds), *Das garantierte Grundeinkommen* (The Guaranteed Basic Income; Frankfurt-am-Main: Fischer Alternativ, 1986); Michael Opielka and Llona Ostner (eds), *Umbau des Sozialstaats* (Reorganization of the Social State; Essen: Klartext, 1987).

14 See, in particular, Les Verts, *Les Verts et l'économie* (The Greens and the Economy; Gentilly: Les Verts, 1992); the periodical *Transversales Science Culture*; and Guy Aznar, *Non aux loisirs, non à la retraite* (No to Leisure. No to Retirement; Paris: Galilée, 1978), *Tous à mi-temps, ou le scénario bleu* (Everyone on Part-Time Working or the Blue Scenario; Paris: Le Seuil, 1981) and *Le Travail, c'est fini. A plein toute la vie* (Work is Over. One's Whole Life on Full Capacity; Paris: Belfond, 1990).

15 See Nordal Akerman, 'Can Sweden be shrunk?', *Development Dialogue*, 2 (1979).

CHAPTER THREE

THE SOCIAL IDEOLOGY OF THE CAR

The really bad thing about cars is that they are like stately homes or villas on the Riviera: luxury goods invented for the exclusive pleasure of a minority of super-rich people, which were in no way, either in their design or in their nature, meant for popular use. Unlike the vacuum cleaner, the wireless or the bicycle, which retain their full use-value when everyone has one, the attractions and advantages of cars, like villas on the Riviera, depend on their being beyond the reach of the masses. This is because, both in design and original purpose, the car is a luxury good. And luxury cannot, by definition, be democratized: if everyone has luxury, then no one has the advantages of luxury. Quite the opposite, in fact. Everyone frustrates and dispossesses others—in short, takes them for a ride. And everyone is, in turn, frustrated, dispossessed and taken for a ride.

The point is usually conceded when it comes to villas on the Riviera. No demagogue has yet dared to claim that democratizing the right to paid holidays meant applying the principle of *one villa with a private beach for every French family*. Everyone can see that if each of the 13 or 14 million families were to have merely 10 metres of coastline, it would take 140,000 kilometres of beach for everyone to have their due! Giving everyone their share means cutting up the beaches into strips so small—or packing the villas so tightly against each other—that their use-value would fall to zero, and the advantage over a hotel complex would disappear altogether. In short, there is only one solution to the democratization of beach access—the collectivist solution. And that solution necessarily involves declaring war on luxury in the form of private beaches, a privilege that a small minority claim for themselves *at everyone else's expense.*

Why is what is perfectly clear in respect of beaches not generally accepted when it comes to transport? Doesn't a car, like a villa with a beach, occupy a *scarce space*? Doesn't it rob other road users (bus/tram passengers, cyclists, pedestrians) of what is rightfully theirs? And when everyone else uses their car, doesn't it totally lose its use-value? Yet there is no shortage of demagogues to assert that every family is entitled to at least one car and that it is the state's job to enable everyone to park as and where they like, to drive through the town as they wish and to set out on the roads *at the same time as everyone else* at weekends and holiday times at 90 miles an hour.

The monstrous nature of such demagoguery is patent to the blindest and yet the Left is not above resorting to it. Why is the car treated as a sacred cow? Why, unlike other 'privative' goods, is it not recognized as an anti-social luxury? We must look for the answer in the two following aspects of motoring.

1. Mass motoring embodies an absolute triumph of bourgeois ideology at the level of everyday practice: it produces—and keeps alive in everyone—the illusory belief that each individual can prevail and gain advantage *over everyone else*. The competitive, aggressive, cruel selfishness of the driver who is, at every moment, symbolically murdering the 'others', whom he sees only as material obstacles and hindrances to his own speed, marks the advent, thanks to daily car-use, of a *universally bourgeois behaviour* (dismayed at the spectacle of Parisian traffic, an East German friend once told me: 'You'll never build socialism with those people').

2. The car provides a self-contradictory example of a luxury object that has been undermined by its own dissemination. But its practical loss of value has not yet led to its ideological devaluation: the myth of the

attractiveness and benefit of car-use persists even though public transport would, if it were more widespread, be manifestly superior. The persistence of this myth is easily explained: the spread of individual motoring has squeezed out public transport, modified town- and country-planning, and transferred to the car those functions that its own dissemination has made necessary. An ideological ('cultural') revolution will be needed to break this circle. There is clearly no point looking to the dominant class (of Right or Left) to provide this.

Let us examine these two points more closely.

When the car was invented, it was intended to procure an entirely novel privilege for a number of very rich bourgeois: the privilege of travelling much faster than everyone else. Up to that point, no one had thought of this: the speed of stagecoaches was more or less the same, whether you were rich or poor; the lord's carriage went no faster than the peasant's cart, and trains carried everyone at the same speed (they adopted differentiated speeds only to meet the competition from cars and aeroplanes). Until the turn of the twentieth century, there wasn't one speed of travel for the elite and another for the general populace. The car would change that: for the first time, it extended class distinction to speed and transport.

The car was so different from ordinary means of transport that it initially seemed inaccessible to the masses: it was not comparable with the cart, the railway train, the bicycle or the horse-drawn omnibus. Exceptional people went around in self-propelled vehicles, weighing the best part of a ton, all of whose—extremely complicated—mechanical parts were the more mysterious for being hidden from sight. For there was also this aspect that weighed heavily in the motoring myth: for the first time, men were astride individual vehicles whose operating mechanisms they in no way understood and which they had to entrust to specialists to maintain and even to fuel.

It was the paradox of the automobile that it apparently conferred unlimited independence on its owners, enabling them to travel at times and along routes of their own choosing at a speed equal to or greater than the railways. In reality, however, this apparent autonomy went hand in hand with a thorough dependency: unlike the horseman, carter or cyclist, the motorist would depend, for his energy supplies, and indeed for the repair of the tiniest damage, on dealers and specialists in carburation, lubrication, ignition and spare parts. Unlike all the previous owners of means of locomotion, the motorist would stand in a relation of *user* and *consumer*, not of *master* and *possessor*, to the vehicle that he formally owned. In other words, this vehicle would oblige him to consume and use a host of commercial services and industrial products which only third parties could provide for him. The apparent autonomy of a car-owner concealed his thorough dependency.

The oil magnates were the first to spot the advantage to be gained from widespread car ownership. If the popular classes could be persuaded to go about in motorized vehicles, you could sell them the energy required for their propulsion. For the first time in history, human beings would become dependent, in their locomotion, on a commercial energy-source. There would be as many customers for the oil industry as there were motorists. And since there would be as many motorists as there were families, the entire population were going to become the clients of the oil producers. The situation every capitalist dreams of was going to become reality: everyone was going to depend, for his daily needs, on a commodity over which a single industry held a monopoly.

All that was needed was to get the general populace to drive cars. It was believed that they were, in most cases, only too willing to do so. All that was needed was to reduce the price of cars sufficiently by mass manufacturing and the use of assembly lines and people would rush to buy them. And, indeed, they did, without realizing that they were being led by the nose. What did the car industry actually promise them? Quite simply this: 'You too will, in future, enjoy the privilege, like aristocrats and the upper middle classes, of driving around more quickly than everyone else. In the car-driving society, the privilege of the elite is within your grasp.'

There was a dash to acquire cars up to the point when, as workers got them in their turn, the frustrated motorists realized they had been duped. They had been promised an upper-middle-class privilege. They had taken on debt to acquire it and suddenly they saw everyone else acquiring this privilege at the same time. And what is a privilege if everyone has it? It was a fool's bargain. Worse than that, they were in a war of each against all. And that general wrangle produced general paralysis, since, when everyone is trying to move at the privileged speed of the upper middle classes, the outcome is that nothing moves at all. The velocity of urban traffic falls, in Boston, Paris, Rome or London, below the speed of the horse-drawn omnibus and the average speed at weekends on the major roads falls below cycling pace.

There is no solution to this: all possible remedies have been tried, but each ends up making the problem worse. Whether they build more radial roads or ring roads, overhead cross-routes or eight-lane toll motorways, the outcome is always the same: the more roads there are, the more cars use them and the greater the paralysis induced by urban traffic congestion. So long as there are towns and cities, the problem will remain unsolved: however broad and fast a distribution road may be, the speed at which vehicles leave it to enter a town cannot be higher than the speed at which they feed into the urban road network. So long as the average speed in Paris remains between six and 12 miles per hour, depending on the time of day, it will not be possible to leave the outer ring road and motorways serving the capital at more than six to 12 miles per hour. And once the exits are saturated, this speed will come down much lower, and there will be a knock-on effect for tens of miles back along the motorway if the approach roads are saturated.

The same goes for any city. It is impossible to travel, on average, at more than 12 miles per hour in the lattice-work of intersecting streets, avenues and boulevards that has, until now, made up our cities. Any injection of vehicles travelling faster disrupts the circulation of the traffic, leading to bottlenecks and, ultimately, gridlock.

If the car is to prevail, only one solution remains and that is to do away with cities altogether or, rather, to stretch them out over hundreds of miles along monumental roadways, as highway suburbs. This is what they have done in the United States. Illich sums up the effect of this in the following startling figures:

> The typical American male devotes more than 1,600 hours a year to his car. He sits in it while it goes and while it stands idling. He parks it and searches for it. He earns the money to put down on it and to meet the monthly instalments. He works to pay for petrol, tolls, insurance, taxes and tickets. He spends four of his sixteen waking hours on the road or gathering his resources for it [. . .] The model American puts in 1,600 hours to get 7,500 miles: less than five miles per hour. In countries deprived of a transportation industry, people manage to do the same, walking wherever they want to go . . . [1]

In non-industrialized countries, adds Illich, travel takes up only three to eight per cent of social time (which probably corresponds to two to six hours per week). He comes to the conclusion, then, that a man on foot covers as many miles per hour as a motorized individual, but that he devotes between five and ten times less time to travelling. The moral of the story: the more widespread rapid vehicles become, the more time (after a certain threshold) people spend—and waste—in travel. This is a mathematical fact.

Why should this be? We have just mentioned the reason: conurbations have been broken up into end-less highway suburbs, since this was the only way of avoiding congestion in the residential centres. But there is an obvious downside to this solution: in the end, people can move around freely only because they are a long way from everything. To make room for the car, distances have been increased. We live a long way from our places of work, schools and supermarkets, which means that a second car will be needed so that the 'housewife' can do the shopping and drive the children to school. As for pleasure trips, they are out of the question. And when it comes to friends, one has the neighbours, if one gets on with them. In the end, cars waste more time than they save and create distance rather than overcoming it. Admittedly, you can drive to your work at 60 miles an hour. But that's because you live 30 miles away and you're willing to waste half an hour over the last six miles. Overall, then, 'people work a substantial part of every day to earn the money without which they could not even get to work' (Illich).[2]

Perhaps you are thinking, 'This way, once the day's work is done, then at least we escape the hell of the city.' So here we have it. The cat is out of the bag. 'The city' is seen now as a 'hell'. All we want to do is escape from it or go and live in the provinces, whereas for generations the city, with all its marvels, was the only place worth living. Why this turnabout? For one reason alone: the car has made cities uninhabitable. It has made them stinking, noisy, suffocating, dusty and crowded, to the point where people no longer want to go out in the evening. And since cars have killed the cities, more and faster cars are needed to escape along the motorways to even further outlying suburbs. There is a perfect circularity to the argument: give us more cars to flee the ravages caused by cars.

Having once been a luxury object and a source of privilege, the car has come to meet a vital need. You need one to get out of the urban hell created by the car. And so capitalist industry has won: what was superfluous has become necessary. There is now no need to persuade people they want a car. The need for one is part of the fabric of life. Admittedly, doubts may arise as you watch the motorized exodus along the escape routes out of the city. Between 8 and 9.30 a.m. and 5.30 and 7 p.m. and for five to six hours at weekends, these escape vehicles stretch out in bumper-to-bumper processions, moving (at best) at the speed of a cyclist and shrouded in a great cloud of leaded petrol. What remains of the advantages of the automobile? What advantages are left when, as was inevitable, the top speed on the roads is limited to precisely what can be achieved by the *slowest* of saloon cars?

There is poetic justice in this: after killing off the city, the car is killing off the car. After promising everyone they would go faster, the car industry has arrived at the entirely foreseeable result that everyone is going slower than the very slowest, at a speed determined by the simple laws of fluid dynamics. Worse than this, having been invented to enable its owners to go where they want, at the time and speed of their own choosing, the car is becoming the most unfree, random, unpredictable and inconvenient of all vehicles. No matter that you choose some outlandish time at which to set off, you never know when the traffic jams will allow you to reach your destination. You are tied to the roads (and motorways) as inexorably as the train to its rails. No more than the rail passenger can you stop on impulse. And, as in a train, you have to advance at a speed set by others. All in all, the car has all the disadvantages of the train—plus a few of its own, such as being shaken about and left feeling stiff, the danger of collision and the need to drive the vehicle—without any of its advantages.

And yet, you will say, people do not take the train. But how in heaven's name would they? Have you tried to go by train from Boston to New York? Or from Ivry to Le Tréport? Or from Garches to Fontainebleau? Or from Colombes to L'Isle-Adam? Have you tried in summer on a Saturday or Sunday? Well, go ahead and the best of luck to you! You will find that automobile capitalism is ahead of the game: at just the point when the car was about to kill off the car, it eliminated the alternative solutions so as to make cars obligatory. The capitalist state first allowed the rail links between cities, their suburbs and the surrounding countryside to fall into disrepair, then got rid of them altogether. The only lines that found favour with it were the high-speed intercity links which compete for middle-class clients with the domestic airlines. The hovertrain, which could have brought the Normandy coast or the lakes of the Morvan within reach of Parisian Sunday picknickers, will actually serve to knock 15 minutes off the journey between Paris and Pontoise and to spew out into its terminuses more speed-saturated passengers than the urban transport system can cope with. There's progress for you!

The truth is that no one really has a choice. You are not free either to have a car or not, because the suburban world is built around it, as, increasingly, is the urban world. This is why the ideal revolutionary solution, which is to abolish the car and replace it with bicycles, trams, buses and driverless taxis, is no longer feasible in the towns and cities structured around motorways, such as Los Angeles, Detroit, Houston, Trappes-en-Yvelines or even Brussels, all of which are shaped by, and built for, the car. These are empty, fragmented places, stretching out along empty streets with their rows of identical houses, where the urban landscape (the urban desert) signals that, 'These streets are made for driving as fast as possible from home to the workplace and vice versa. This is somewhere you pass through, not somewhere to stop. Once everyone has finished work, they are expected to stay home. Anyone found in the streets after nightfall must be suspected of being up to no good.' And indeed, in some

American cities, the fact of strolling around the streets at night is regarded as an offence.

So is the game up? It is not, but the alternative to the car will necessarily entail a comprehensive rethink. If people are going to be *able* to give up *their* cars, it isn't enough merely to offer them more convenient forms of public transport. They will have to be able to do without transport altogether because they feel at home in their own part of town, their municipality or human-scale city, and *because they enjoy walking home from their place of work*—walking or, at a pinch, cycling. No rapid, escapist means of transport will ever make up for the misery of living in an uninhabitable city, not feeling at home anywhere, and merely *passing through* to work or, alternatively, to cut oneself off from the world and sleep.

'The people who now call themselves rich,' writes Illich, 'would break with bondage to overefficient transport on the day they came to treasure the horizon of their traffic islands, now fully grown, and to dread frequent shipments from their homes.'[3] But this is just the point. In order to be able to love one's home ground, it will first have to be made liveable, not driveable: the area or district will have to become once again the microcosm shaped by and for all human activities, in which people live, work, relax, learn, communicate, knock around and together co-manage their shared environment. When they asked Marcuse once what people would do with their time after the revolution, when capitalist waste was abolished, he replied, 'We're going to destroy the big cities and build new ones. That will keep us busy for a while.'

We may imagine these new cities as federations of municipalities (or districts) surrounded by 'green belts', in which the residents—and the schoolchildren, in particular—will spend several hours a week growing the fresh produce required to feed them. For their daily travel, they will have available to them a complete range of means of transport suited to an average town: municipal bicycles, trams or trolleybuses and driverless electric taxis. For longer trips in the countryside and for transporting guests, a pool of communal automobiles will be at everyone's disposal in the area's garages. The car will no longer be a need. Everything will have changed: life, the world, people. And it will not have come about all by itself.

Meanwhile, how are we to get to that point? Above all, we mustn't pose the problem of transport in isolation. It must always be linked to the problems of urban space, the social division of labour and the compartmentalization between the various dimensions of existence this has introduced, in which there is one place for working, another for 'living', a third for obtaining supplies, a fourth for learning and a fifth for entertainment. The arrangement of space is a continuation of the splintering of human beings that began with the division of labour in the factory. It slices individuals up, cutting their time and life into separate slices, so that in each slice you are a passive consumer, handed over defenceless to the salesmen, with the result that it never occurs to you that work, culture, communication, pleasure, the satisfaction of needs and your personal life can and should be one and the same thing: the unity of a life, sustained by the social fabric of the town where you live.

Notes

1 Ivan Illich, *Energy and Equity* (Worcester and London: The Trinity Press, 1974).

2 Ivan Illich, *Toward a History of Needs* (New York: Pantheon Books, 1978), p. 127.

3 Ibid., p. 142.

CHAPTER FOUR

DESTRUCTIVE GROWTH
AND THE PRODUCTIVE ALTERNATIVE

Since the early 1960s, we have leaned, in all our social and economic options, towards manufacturing processes and consumer goods with a high energy content. In the construction industry, stone and brick have been replaced by concrete, steel and aluminium; leather has been replaced by plastics; returnable glass containers have been replaced by throw-away packaging, natural fibres by synthetic fibres, public transport by individual vehicles, average-sized towns by vast suburban sprawl around cities, organic fertilizers by synthetic ones, etc.

At the same time, the lifespan of products has been artificially reduced. Among other things, nylon is now put through a process that makes it more fragile; so-called consumer durables are designed not to last on average more than seven years; many machines are designed so that they cannot be repaired; most sheet metals are corrosion-proofed inadequately or not at all; refrigerators are poorly insulated and consume twice as much electricity as they did 15 years ago; washing machines consume three times as much energy as is necessary and wear out clothing more quickly than would a rationally adjusted machine.[1]

These instances of waste have enabled capitalism to secure a return on ever greater quantities of capital by increasing the volume of consumption (and production) to a fantastic degree. For consumers, this increase in the volume of goods has often been a fool's bargain: they are forced to buy a greater volume of goods to obtain the same degree of use-value.

This trend is reflected in the figures: to increase GDP by one per cent, almost twice as much energy was needed after 1965 as was required 15 years earlier.

SOME ENERGY COSTS

To obtain a ton of the products below, a quantity of energy has to be expended which, expressed in tons of oil equivalent (TOE) represents between 10 per cent and 590 per cent of the weight of the product.

PRODUCT IN TONS	ENERGY COST (IN TOE)
Synthetic fabric	5.9
Aluminium foil	5.8
Newly smelted aluminium	5.1
Recycled aluminium	0.18
Polystyrene	3.7
Other plastics	1.7–2.1
Asbestos cement	1.4
Ammonia	0.96
Glass windows	0.6
Steel	0.5–0.7
Paper	0.46–0.48

Cement	0.116
Bricks	0.075
Plaster	0.056

Overall, present levels of energy consumption do not reflect specific needs that cannot be reduced but the choice of a certain kind of development specific to 'affluent' capitalism: this consists in creating the greatest possible number of needs and satisfying them in a makeshift way with the greatest possible quantity of commodities. It consists in replacing simple tools and machines with complex and excessively powerful novelties; in inventing, as soon as everyone has gained access to a particular device, some new piece of equipment consuming more energy than the preceding ones. The higher one moves up the salary ladder, the greater the incentive to satisfy one's desires through high energy consumption when they could be satisfied in other ways: the level of energy consumption has become, willy-nilly, a matter of social status.

This is clearly the case with transport: the power of one's car is a symbol of wealth; in a single Paris–Washington return flight, the Concorde passenger consumes as much energy as the average French person in a year. It is less clear, but equally true of domestic equipment: *electric* cookers, freezers, air-conditioning systems, dishwashers and *electric* boilers, which are expensive machines and, by their very design, wasteful of energy, have replaced less costly and sophisticated machinery of at least equal use-value.

> For many years now, we have not been buying clothes, but fashion or respectability. The public no longer buys products; they buy satisfactions or meanings [. . .] In this new context, the key thing is to create difference, not equivalence, to invent the new service that wins out by its attractiveness and the meanings with which it is laden: power, esteem, safety, good taste, happiness.[2]

Official forecasts always assume that these trends towards wastefulness will continue: they tell us that household energy consumption will continue to rise by seven per cent per year, consumption of bottles by nine per cent, of plastics by seventeen per cent, of cement by five per cent, etc. In 20 years' time, we are told, we shall consume two-and-a-half to three times as much energy, commodities and services as we do now.

Do we need these purchases? Do we *desire* them? Do they enable us to achieve fulfilment, to communicate, to have a more relaxed lifestyle or more fraternal relations? Economic forecasting knows nothing of these questions: it records the trends at work and projects them into the future as though they were immutable facts. It puts its trust in the producers of goods and services to make us consume three times as much as we do now. They will manufacture the corresponding needs. They will invent new shortages and wants, new forms of luxury and poverty. They will manufacture these things deliberately and systematically, in keeping with their needs for profitability and growth. They have in their service sales promotion strategists who will be able to manipulate our most secret motives to make their products irresistible through the symbols with which they freight them.

Twenty years ago, one of these strategists candidly let the cat out of the bag. His name is Stanley Resor, the president of J. Walter Thompson, the biggest advertising agency in the United States. He said:

> When incomes rise, the most important thing is the creation of new needs. When you ask people, 'Do you know that your standard of living will increase by 50% over 10 years?', they haven't the faintest idea what that means [. . .] They don't feel the need for a second car unless you remind them forcefully of the fact. This need has to be created in their minds and you have to make them realize the advantages a second car will bring them. At times they are even hostile to the idea. I see advertising as the educative, activating force capable of bringing about the changes in demand that we need. By teaching many people a higher standard of living, it increases consumption to a level commensurate with our productivity and resources.[3]

This tells us all we need to know: the consumer exists to serve production; he must provide it with the outlets it demands; he must have the needs that are required for the most profitable sales to expand. We shall be given these needs. We shall have to be if society is to perpetuate itself, if its inequalities are to be reproduced and its mechanisms of domination to remain in place.

The consumption forecasts that guide economic activity are always based on this hypothesis: society will not change profoundly, nor will the way of producing, consuming and living. There will always be poor and rich, people who obey and others who command, underground trains for which we queue and half-empty Concordes. We shall go on living hurried lives; having neither the time nor the inclination for autonomous activities. We shall not have the desire or the power to reflect on our needs, to debate with others the best ways to satisfy them and to define the corresponding collective options freely.

Economic forecasting is not, then, neutral. It reflects the tacit political choice to perpetuate the current system. This has nothing to do with objectivity or scientific rigour. Present society is not the only possible society and its mode of operation is, in no sense, an objective necessity.

We are perfectly entitled to reject the official forecasts and the necessities that flow from them. But we have to be aware that this rejection is a rejection of the existing social order, a political rejection. The idea that production and consumption can be decided on the basis of needs is politically subversive. It presupposes that those who produce and those who consume can get together, reflect among themselves and decide freely. This assumes a society in which the decision-making power of capital and/or the state with regard to investment, production, innovation and trade policy is abolished. It assumes, in short, a form of economic management in which the aim is to satisfy *the greatest possible number* of needs with *the smallest possible amount* of labour, capital and physical resources.

That aim is the radical negation of capitalist logic. Entailed in it is the desire to achieve the maximum of satisfaction with the minimum of production. Such a pursuit of maximum efficiency, and hence of optimum economy, is so totally foreign to capitalist logic that macroeconomic theory is not even capable of registering savings of effort in its accounts. Whereas, in common parlance, to make 'economies' is to *avoid* consumption and production, and hence to gain time and effort by more efficient management, in the national accounting statistics these savings appear as *losses*, as reductions in GDP, as decreases in the volume of goods and services available to the population.

We discover here how skewed the official methods of forecasting and calculation are. They count any growth in production and purchases as an increase in national wealth—including the increasing production of disposable packaging, machinery and metals thrown into dumps, paper burned with the household waste, utensils that are broken and beyond repair, medical care and artificial limbs for those injured at work or on the roads. In this way, things destroyed appear as sources of wealth, since everything that is broken, scrapped or lost will have to be replaced and will give rise to the production and sale of commodities, to flows of money, to profits. The quicker things break, wear out, go out of fashion or are thrown away, the higher the GDP and the more the nation's accountants will tell us we are rich. Even illness and injuries are counted as sources of enrichment, insofar as they increase the consumption of medicines and treatment.

But if the opposite happens, if good health saves us medical expenditure, if the things we buy last half a lifetime, without going out of fashion or deteriorating, if they can be repaired and even easily transformed, then of course the GDP will fall: we shall work fewer hours, consume less and have fewer needs.

How do we replace an economic system based on the pursuit of maximum waste with an economic system based on keeping that waste to a minimum? The question is more than a century old; it is the very question of the replacement of capitalism by socialism, for only socialism—that is to say, only a way of production freed from the imperative of maximum profit and managed in the interest of all and by all who contribute to it—can afford itself the luxury of pursuing the greatest satisfaction at the lowest possible cost. It alone can break with the logic of maximum profit, maximum wastage, maximum production and consumption, and replace it with economic good sense: maximum satisfaction with minimum expenditure. Only socialism can invest today so as to save tomorrow. In other words, only socialism can invest with a view to selling a lesser volume of more durable products on which the profits, as currently conceived, would also be lower.

In actual fact, the use of the term 'socialism' is inappropriate here. We should speak, rather, of Communism—that is to say, of a stage at which the 'full development of the productive forces' is already achieved and in which the main task is no longer maximum production, nor the employment of everyone, but a different organization of the economy in which full-time work is no longer the precondition for a full income or, to put it another way, in which covering everyone's needs is assured in exchange for a quantity of social labour that occupies only a small part of everyone's time.

We have virtually arrived at this stage. The full satisfaction of all needs in exchange for the perform-ance of less work is not prevented by the forces or means of production being insufficiently developed, but rather by their being over-developed. The system has been able to grow and reproduce itself only by accelerating the destruction of commodities along-side their production; by organizing new forms of scarcity as the mass of wealth was increasing; by de-valorizing the elements of that wealth when they were in danger of becoming accessible to all; and, in this way, perpetuating poverty alongside privilege and frus-tration alongside affluence.

In other words, the development of the produc-tive forces within the framework of capitalism will never lead to the gates of Communism, since the technologies, the relations of production and the nature of the products exclude not just the durable, equitable satisfaction of needs but also the stabilization of social production at a level commonly accepted as *sufficient*. The very idea that there may one day be *enough* for each and all—and hence that the pursuit of 'more' and 'better' can give way to the pursuit of extra-economic, non-commodity values—is alien to capitalist society. It is, on the other hand, essential to Communism and that system will be able to take shape as a positive negation of the dominant system only if the ideas of self-limitation, stabilization, fairness and free availability find a practical illustration— that is to say, if it is practically demonstrated that not only can one live better by working and consuming less and differently, but that this voluntary, collective limitation of the sphere of necessity can, as of now— alone—make possible an extension of the sphere of autonomy or, in other words, of freedom.

'Enough!' writes Roger-Gérard Schwartzenberg. 'According to a survey carried out in 1975 by the Norwegian Government Food Institute, 76 per cent of Norwegians are dissatisfied: they are, in fact, of the opinion that the living standard of their country is "too high". The great majority of those questioned would prefer "a simple, quiet life, with just the necessary amount of things". They would like "incomes and careerism to be limited".[4]

Hence, the importance of 'social experimentation' around new ways of living communally, of consuming, producing and distributing. Hence, too, the importance of alternative technologies, enabling us to do more and better with less, whether these technologies are developed by grassroots communities, municipal authorities or even—within necessarily narrow limits, so long as we remain within the framework of the current system—state initiative.

DOING BETTER . . .

The best products are those which give the longest satisfaction and enable us, by their aesthetic qualities, to become attached to them.

The best products are:

> the longest-lasting;
> the easiest to repair and maintain;
> the easiest to dismantle at the end of their lifespan so that the metals can be recovered;
> those which consume least energy for the same level of performance.

Incentives

> Lower VAT on durable products;
> Indication of lifespan alongside price;
> Instructions describing the most common repairs, with an indication of how long they take and how much they cost;
> All machinery to carry a notice of its energy consumption.

. . . WITH LESS

Shared usage enables us to obtain equipment that lies beyond the resources of a single household. It can also enable individuals and the community to make very substantial savings.

Equipment to be provided in every new apartment

building and, in older neighbourhoods, every block of houses:

> a laundry/wash-house;
> a place for drying washing, heated by the hot water system;
> a workshop;
> a play area for children (and adults);
> a TV, film-projection and music room.

The state, like capital, is in fact perfectly capable of promoting certain alternative technologies and certain forms of energy- and resource-saving right now. The meaning of state initiatives in this field is clearly very different, in the present conditions, from 'social experimentation': it is the function of such initiatives to facilitate *by another route* the expansion of heavy technologies and new forms of social control and domination.

The fact that certain state initiatives have been co-opted into the service of capital should not, however, lead to their being condemned out of hand, nor to the belief that a break with the present system will be crowned by a complete disappearance of the state.

On the contrary, current initiatives on alternative technologies are deserving of a critique that encompasses both what they reveal and what they hide. They reveal possible alternatives to the current model of development, while at the same time striving to mask those alternatives. French state programmes on solar energy, for example, reveal both the technical and economic feasibility of decentralized energy production at neighbourhood, municipality or household level, and the refusal of the state to exploit these technologies.

The fact that they are mainly being developed by activist groups as essential tools for a societal alternative does not mean that that alternative can win out in the absence of any political mediation. If the time individuals spend producing everything necessary is to be reduced to a minimum, as is their dependence on random factors and circumstances of a local order, then the socialization of the production of necessary goods and the central regulation of distribution and exchange remain essential. The sphere of necessity—and hence of socially necessary labour time—can be reduced to a minimum only by as effective as possible a coordination and regulation of flows and stocks—that is to say, by flexible planning. The social income for life that would be paid to everyone in exchange for 20,000 hours of socially useful labour—which every citizen would be free to divide up into as many fractions as she likes, continuously or discontinuously, in one field or a range of fields—is possible only if there is a central organ of regulation and *payment* or, in other words, a state.

Hence, the answer to the capitalist system is neither a return to the household economy and village autarky, nor the total, planned socialization of all activities: it consists, rather, in socializing the sphere of necessity alone, in order to *reduce to a minimum*, within everyone's life, what needs to be done, whether we like it or not, and *extend to the maximum* the sphere of freedom or, in other words, the sphere of autonomous—individual or collective—activities performed for their own sake.

Both the state totally taking over individuals, and individuals taking the needs of society's overall operation upon themselves are things that have to be rejected. The identification of the individual with the state and the identification of the demands of the state with individual happiness are the two faces of totalitarianism.

The sphere of necessity and the sphere of liberty do not overlap. Marx himself reasserted this at the end of *Volume 3* of *Capital*. For this very reason, the expansion of the sphere of liberty requires that the sphere of necessity be clearly delimited. The only function of a Communist state is to manage the sphere of necessity (which is also that of socialized needs) in such a way that it is continually shrinking and making available growing spaces of autonomy.

Notes

1 See Adret, *Travailler deux heures par jour* (Work Two Hours a Day; Paris: Le Seuil, 1979).

2 Marcel Boiteux, the Director-General of EDF, speaking to the French Academy of Commercial Sciences on 20 March 1972.

3 Quoted in André Gorz, *La Morale de l'histoire* (The Morality of History; Paris: Le Seuil, 1959).

4 Roger-Gérard Schwartzenberg, *Socialisme politique* (Political Socialism; 3rd edn; Paris: Montchrestien, 1977), p. 392.

CHAPTER FIVE

GLOBAL CRISIS, DE-GROWTH
AND THE EXIT FROM CAPITALISM

In memoriam
Jean-Marie Vincent

De-growth is a good idea: it indicates the direction in which we must go and invites us to imagine how to live better while consuming and working less and differently. But this good idea can find no political expression; no government would dare implement it, none of the economic actors would accept it, unless its implementation were fragmented into measures subordinate to other imperatives, stretched out over one or more decades, and were thus emptied of its radical potential and made compatible with the perpetuation of the dominant economic system.

What must 'de-grow', in fact, is the production of commodities, which is already too straitened and sparing of human labour to enable the over-abundance of capital to valorize itself. De-growth would cause a severe economic depression, if not indeed the collapse of the global banking system. To stretch it out over one or more decades would assume that the dominant economic system is certain to endure. For several reasons, this is not the case.

For 20 years, capitalism has been sinking into a crisis that leaves no way out. It is approaching (I shall come back to this) its internal limit, its extinction. The causes of this crisis are the IT revolution, the dematerialization of labour and capital, and the increasing impossibility of measuring the value of either (or the value of commodities) that ensues from this.

Employment statistics should not deceive us as to the fact that the productivity of labour is continuing to rise rapidly and the volume of 'productive work'—in the sense this term has in a capitalist economy—to diminish dramatically. In that economy, only work that 'valorizes' (that is to say, increases) capital is 'productive', because the person who performs that work does not consume all the 'value' of what he has produced. Personal services, in particular, are unproductive from this standpoint. In the United States, often cited as a model, these occupy 55 per cent of the active population, who work as waiters/waitresses, salespeople, cleaners, domestic help, janitors, nannies, etc. Half of that population have several insecure jobs; a quarter of them figure among the 'working poor'. These jobs do not increase the quantity of means of payment in circulation: they do not create 'value'. The remuneration of this work comes out of incomes from productive work: it is a secondary income. The directly capital-productive population represents probably less than 10 per cent of the working population of the so-called developed countries.[1] Ignacio Ramonet cites a very eloquent figure on this subject: more than 25 per cent of global economic activity is performed by 200 multinationals, which employ 0.75 per cent of the world's population.

The more the productivity of labour increases, the lower the number of workers on whom the valorization of a given volume of capital depends. To prevent the volume of profit from falling, the productivity of an ever-decreasing working population would have to increase more quickly.[2] Capitalism runs up against its internal limit when the number of capital-productive workers falls so low that capital is no longer able to reproduce itself and profit collapses.[3] This limit has virtually been reached, as has the external limit—that is to say, the impossibility of finding profitable outlets for a volume of commodities that should grow *at least* as quickly as productivity. Each firm seeks to push back these two limits for itself by waging a war of annihilation on its competitors and by seeking to carve them up, so as to appropriate their marketable assets and their market share. There are more and more losers and fewer and fewer winners. The record profits the winners achieve mask the fact that the mass of profit overall is decreasing. A significant proportion of these record profits is not reinvested in production, which is not sufficiently profitable. The 500 firms in the Standard & Poor's Index have between them 631 billion dollars of reserves. A study by the management consultants McKinsey estimates that the amount of capital in search of investment opportunities is 800 trillion dollars. More than half of American companies' profits derive from financial operations. In order to reproduce itself and grow, capital is resorting less and less to the production of commodities and more and more to the 'financial industry', which produces nothing. In fact, that industry 'creates' money with money; it creates money without substance by buying and selling financial assets and fuelling speculative bubbles. These develop thanks to speculative purchases of assets such as shares, including shares in property/land companies, or funds that speculate on prices of metals or currencies, etc. The purchases push up the prices of shares in investment trusts and create a speculative movement that accelerates that rise. The continuous increase in the prices of securities enables their holders to borrow increasing sums from the banks. These sums, used for other speculative investments or for the purchase of goods, give the impression that the economy has a high level of liquidity. This is due, in reality, to a vertiginous growth in debts of all kinds, which are underwritten by the over-inflated prices of the securities that are part of the bubble. The latest of these, the property bubble, described by *The Economist* as 'the biggest speculative bubble of all time', has pushed up the 'value' of the industrialized world's real estate from 20 to 60 trillion dollars in three years.

Every bubble ends up bursting sooner or later, at which point it transforms the merely notional financial assets in the banks' balance sheets into debts. Unless it is replaced by a new, even larger bubble, the bursting of a bubble normally entails serial bankruptcies—and ultimately, the collapse of the global banking system.[4]

The valorization of capital depends increasingly on artifice and decreasingly on the production and sale of commodities. The wealth produced decreasingly assumes the value-form or commodity form; it is less and less measurable in terms of exchange-value and GDP. Several factors are showing up the fragility of the system—the crisis it is in—and pointing towards a fundamentally different economy that is no longer governed by capital's need to expand and the general concern to 'make' and 'earn' money, but by a concern that the forces of life and creativity should blossom, that is to say, a concern with the sources of true wealth which can neither be expressed nor measured in terms of monetary value.[5]

The contraction of the economy based on exchange-value is already taking place and will become more pronounced. The question is simply whether it is going to take the form of a catastrophic crisis that we passively undergo, or a self-organized societal choice, founding an economy and civilization beyond wage-labour and commodity relations, its seeds having been sown and its tools forged by persuasive forms of social experimentation.

We have to be very clear here—we shall always have as much work as we want, but it will no longer take the form of employment/commodity-labour. It is not just full employment, but employment itself that post-Fordism has undertaken to eliminate. By that elimination, capitalism contributes to its own extinction and produces unprecedented opportunities to move to an economy freed from the domination by capital of our mode of life, our needs and the way of satisfying them.

It is this domination that remains the insurmountable obstacle to the limiting of production and consumption. It has led to our producing nothing of what we consume and consuming nothing of what we produce. All our needs and desires are needs and desires for commodities, and hence needs for money. We produce wealth in the form of money, which is, by its essence, abstract and limitless; hence, our desire is also limitless. The idea of the *sufficient*—the idea of a limit beyond which we would be producing or buying too much or, in other words, more than we need—forms no part of economics or the economic imagination.

We are incapable of deciding—or even of asking ourselves—*what* we need, either quantitatively or qualitatively. Our desires and needs are severed from us, formatted and impoverished by the omnipresence of commercial propaganda and the excess of commodities. Being commodities ourselves—inasmuch as we now have to 'sell ourselves' to be able to sell our labour—we have internalized the logic specific to capitalism. For that system, *what* is produced is important only insofar as it yields a return; for us, as sellers of our labour, what is produced is important only insofar as it creates employment and distributes wages. Workers and capital are bound by a structural complicity: for each, the crucial goal is to 'earn money'— and as much money as possible. Both regard 'growth' as an essential way of achieving that goal. Both are subject to the immanent constraint of the 'always more', 'always quicker'.

In order to be able to self-determine our needs and agree on the ways and means of satisfying them, it is essential, then, that we regain control of the means of labour and of production decisions. Such control is, however, impossible in an industrialized economy. It is excluded by the very design of the means of production. These require a specialization, subdivision and hierarchization of tasks; they are not neutral technologies, but means of capital's domination of labour. It is the fact that relations of domination are inherent in the industrial mode of production—which remains structurally a capitalism even when industry is 'collectivized'—that explains the persistence of nostalgic utopias that link de-growth, de-industrialization and a return to largely autarkic village, communal and/or family economies in which production is essentially craft production.

However, the possibility of a quite different simultaneous exit from industrialism and capitalism is currently emerging. Capitalism itself is working involuntarily towards its own extinction by developing the tools for a kind of high-tech craft production that make it possible to manufacture almost any three-dimensional objects with a much higher level of productivity than industry and with a minimal consumption of natural resources. I am referring to devices currently used in industry for 'rapid prototyping'—the so-called 'digital fabricators', also known as 'factories in a box', 'personal fabricators' or 'fabbers'. These can be installed in a garage or a workshop, and moved around in an estate car. They use fine powders of resin or metals as their raw material and all it takes to operate them is the design of software programmes that control the fabrication process using lasers. They would enable groups that are excluded or doomed to inactivity or underemployment by the 'development' of capitalism to come together in communal workshops to produce everything they and their communities need.[6]

They offer the possibility of interconnecting communal workshops the world over; of treating software—as the free software movement does—as shared human property; of replacing the market and commodity relations by negotiated agreement about what should be produced, and how, and to what end; of manufacturing all that is necessary locally; and even of building large and complex plants through the co-operation of several dozen local workshops. Transport, warehousing, marketing and factory assembly, which represent two thirds or more of current costs, would be eliminated. An economy beyond 'employment', money and commodities, based on the pooling of the products of an activity originally conceived as shared—a zero-cost economy—begins to seem possible.

Is this the end of work? On the contrary, it is the end of the tyranny exerted by commodity relations over work in the anthropological sense. Work can now free itself from 'external necessities' (Marx), recover its autonomy and turn towards the effectuation of everything that has no price and cannot be bought or sold. It can become that which we do because we really want to do it, and because we find our fulfilment in the activity itself as much as in its outcome. The great question is: what do we want to do in—and make of—our lives? It is a question that the economistic 'more-is-better' culture prevents us from asking and that a third of Frithjof Bergmann's book seeks to teach us to confront.[7]

This is, of course, a utopia. But it is a concrete utopia. It represents an extension of the free software movement, which sees itself as a germinal form of economy of zero cost and pooled resources or, in other words, of a communism. And it chimes with the prospect of an ever more complete elimination of 'employment' and an increasing level of automation, which will make (and is already making) software design by far the most important productive activity—productive of wealth, but not of 'value'.

The so-called underdeveloped or 'developing' world will not save capitalism—nor save itself—by an industrialization generative of full employment. The same logic that led the industrialized world to render its labour force useless and replace it with increasingly efficient robots applies—and will apply—to the so-called emerging nations which, if they are to become and remain competitive and equip themselves with the necessary infrastructures, will have to equal the most advanced economies in productivity. Full employment of the Fordist type is not reproducible by digital post-Fordism.

It is no accident that Robert Kurz's prophetic work *Der Kollaps der Modernisierung* (1994) has become something of a best-seller in Brazil.[8] Nor that it is in South Africa that the projected introduction of 'fab-bers' by Bergmann is welcomed with interest by the ANC.

Of course, the utopia I have shared for many years with Bergmann, which is a utopia of cooperative communal self-providing, is not immediately realiz-able on a grand scale. But as soon as it is implemented at some point on the globe, it will stand as an exem-plary piece of social experimentation. It will offer us a goal that does not involve starting out from the piti-ful make-do-and-mend that is immediately possible, but from the possibility of a radically different world which we now have the means genuinely to wish for. It will contribute to changing our view of what *is* by illustrating what *can be*; it will help us to overthrow the centrality in everyone's consciousness, thinking and imagination of that 'work' which capitalism is abolishing on a massive scale, while at the same time demanding that everyone fight everyone else to obtain it at all costs. It will show up clearly that work is not something that you *have* insofar as someone *gives* it to you, but something that you *do*, provided that you have the means to do it; and that those means, which are also the means for reclaiming work, are now becoming available.

Notes

1 In *Les Aventures de la marchandise. Pour une nouvelle critique de la valeur* (The Adventures of the Commodity. For a New Critique of Value; Paris: Denoël, 2003, pp. 153–5), Anselme Jappe shows that a decreasing proportion of the activities that go on in the world 'create surplus-

value and continue to fuel capitalism'. Upstream, down-stream, and alongside the 'genuine productive process', productive activity needs support from greater and greater quantities of non-productive work, 'which often cannot obey the law of value'. 'For labour to be productive, its products have to feed back into the process of capital accumulation and the consumption of those products has to contribute to the expanded reproduction of capital by being consumed by productive workers or by becoming investment goods.'

2 See Moishe Postone, *Time, Labor and Social Domination. A Reinterpretation of Marx's Critical Theory* (Cambridge: Cambridge University Press, 1993), pp. 308–14. This masterwork by Postone has played an important role in the critique of work and value, and in the distinction between value and wealth within the school of Robert Kurz in particular.

3 For a complete, up-to-date analysis of this, see Robert Kurz, *Das Weltkapital. Globalisierung und inneres Schranken des modernen warenproduzierenden Systems* (Global Capital. Globalization and the Internal Limitation of the Modern, Commodity-Producing System; Berlin: Tiamat, 2005).

4 On the central role of financial bubbles for the apparent survival of the system, see Kurz, *Das Weltkapital*, pp. 228–67 and Robert Brenner, 'New Boom or New Bubble?', *New Left Review*, 25 (January–February 2004).

5 The idea that the growth of the trade in goods—that is to say, the growth of GDP—does not of itself lead to an increase in wealth, but may indicate an impoverishment and deterioration of social relations, is now a widely accepted fact, thanks *inter alia* to the United Nations Development Programme Report of 1998, Dominique Méda's book *Qu'est-ce que la richesse?* (What is Wealth?; Paris: Aubier, 1999) and Patrick Viveret's *Reconsidérer la richesse* (Reconsidering Wealth; Paris: Éditions de l'Aube, 2003). Less widely accepted is the fact that breaking with an economy that measures wealth in monetary terms entails breaking with 'value' in its three forms: money, 'employment' and commodities. Only an economy freed from the law of value can enable production to take place in the service of human development, instead of human beings serving the production of commodities. See Gorz, *L'Immatériel*, pp. 81–8.

6 Digital fabricators or 'fabbers' are, to my knowledge, the most advanced tools industry currently possesses. Tens of pages can be found on their operation, their development, and their current and potential applications on two main websites: www.fabbers.com and www.ennex.com./~fabbers.

A presentation stressing the politico-economic significance of the phenomenon can be found in an article by Stefen Merten and Stefen Meretz, the founders of

Oekonux, entitled 'Freie Software und freie Gesellschaft', at www.opentheory.org/ox_osjahrbuch_ 2005/. The authors present 'fabbers' both as machines that do not enslave human beings to their demands— and are hence no longer instruments of domination— and as robotic devices that are not limited to automating a determinate labour process—practically any process can be programmed on one and the same machine. This prefigures the possibility of an 'information society' in which the whole of human energy can be expended on creative activities 'for the limitless development of the human faculties'. A presentation stressing the practical potentialities of personal fabricators can be found in Chapter 4 of Frithjof Bergmann's *New Work, New Culture* (currently available only in its German version *Neue Arbeit, Neue Kultur*, Freiburg: Arbor Verlag, 2004). Bergmann has been trying for 20 years to transform mass unemployment, which he has seen in Detroit, into an opportunity to 'liberate work from the tyranny of employment'. In other words, instead of having to sell one's labour, one would be able to work and produce according to one's needs in the most satisfying way possible. This required, at the outset, that the products meeting the commonest needs should be redefined so that they could be manufactured with tools and skills that are within everyone's scope. It was the aim of 'high-tech self-providing (HTSP)' to enable both the unemployed of Michigan and Africans in Botswana to meet their needs using the means available to them. Digital fabricators—and Bergmann seems to have won inventors over to the idea—offered the ideal solution.

7 The zero-cost economy is an anti-economy: a very largely demonetarized economy that is no longer governed by the criteria of profitability of business economics, but by the criterion of the 'usefulness' and desirability of products and by consideration of negative and positive externalities that are impossible to evaluate in monetary terms. We find this battle against economism in the writings of Serge Latouche, in the free software movement and, most recently, in the extraordinarily fertile work by Laurence Baranski and Jacques Robin, *L'Urgence de la métamorphose* (The Urgency of Transformation; Paris: Des Idées et des Hommes, 2006), pp. 85–93. See especially the chapter 'Art de vivre et gratuité'.

8 Robert Kurz, *Der Kollaps des Modernisierung. Vom Zusammenbruch des Kasernensozialismus zur Krise der Weltökonomie* (The Collapse of Modernization. From the Fall of Barracks Socialism to the Crisis of the Global Economy; Leipzig: Reclam, 1994). See, in particular, pp. 310–14,

which deals with the need for demonetarization, the impossibility of having individual reproduction depend
on occupying a job subject to the abstract imperatives
of business economics, communal self-providing cooperatives and the international (self) organization of
resource flows de-coupled from the logic of money and
commodities.

CHAPTER SIX

WEALTH WITHOUT VALUE, VALUE WITHOUT WEALTH

SONIA MONTAÑO: *Like many other countries, Brazil is seriously affected by the problem of unemployment. One of the solutions most widely advocated by governments, politicians and economists is renewed growth. But you say that isn't enough. Why not?*

ANDRÉ GORZ: We have first to ask what kind of growth we need. What are we lacking that growth can bring? But these questions are never asked any more.

Economists, governments and businessmen call for *growth* in itself, without ever defining its purpose. Decision-makers aren't interested in the content of growth any more. What interests them is the increase in GDP or, in other words, an increase in the quantity of commodities exchanged and sold over a year, whatever those commodities may be. There's no guarantee that growth in GDP will increase the availability of products that the population needs. In actual fact, this growth is a response to a need first and foremost on the part of capital, not the needs of the population. It often creates more poor people and more poverty. Above all, it advantages a minority at the expense of the majority. It worsens the quality of life and of the environment rather than improving them.

What wealth and resources are populations most often short of? First, a healthy, balanced diet, high-quality drinking water, clean air, light and space, and pleasant, salubrious housing. But the GDP figures don't measure any of that. Let's take an example: a village digs a well and everyone can get their water from it. Water's a shared good and the well's the product of shared work. It's the source of greater wealth for the community. But it doesn't increase the GDP because it doesn't give rise to any monetary exchange: nothing's bought or sold. Yet if the well is dug and appropriated by a private entrepreneur who asks each of the villagers to pay for the water they take from it, GDP will increase by the amounts received by the owner.

Let's take the example of landless peasants. If you distribute uncultivated lands to 100,000 families, and they produce enough to live on from those lands, the GDP doesn't change. It also doesn't change if those families share out the tasks that need to be performed for the general good, and exchange products and services on a mutualistic, cooperative basis. On the other hand, if 100 landowners expel 100,000 families from their lands and grow commercial crops for export, GDP increases by the sum total of these exports, plus the poverty wages paid to the agricultural workers.

GDP recognizes and measures wealth only when it takes the form of commodities. It recognizes as productive work only work sold to an enterprise that makes a profit from it—in other words, an enterprise that can sell on the product of that work at a profit. From capital's point of view, only work that produces a surplus—a 'surplus-value'—that can increase capital is seen as productive.

In countries where the great majority of the population are poor, there are few people you can sell to at a profit. The development of a market economy that can create jobs can be begun only if there's a political power capable of locating its public initiatives and drives within a strategy of exports and development. That power existed in Japan and South Korea, among others. But we must remember, too, that the development of industrial capitalism in those countries took place before neo-liberal globalization, before the microcomputer revolution, and in a period characterized by sustained growth among the northern economies. The markets of the rich countries were expanding, their economies were importing foreign labour and first Japanese, then Korean, industries were able to carve out a place for themselves in the European and North American markets with no great difficulty, provided that they chose their industrialization strategy well.

But, since the end of the 1970s, conditions have changed fundamentally. For a whole range of reasons, exports to the rich countries can no longer be the main engine of growth of the southern economies. First, the northern markets are no longer expanding. Second, neo-liberal globalization no longer allows the so-called emerging countries to protect their domestic industries and agriculture from competition from the northern countries. By opening themselves up to those countries to attract foreign investment, they fall into a fearsome trap. Imports from the North ruin millions of semi-artisanal small enterprises and create industries that provide relatively few jobs and impose heavy 'modernization costs' on the country. The age of the so-called labour-intensive industries is coming to an end. Low wages in the southern countries are no longer sufficient to win them market share. Practically all industrial production now demands a high intensity of capital—hence, substantial investment—and the amortization, remuneration and continual technical modernization of the fixed capital have much more impact on cost prices than do labour costs. The relatively small labour force must have a very high level of productivity, since the profitability of the investment depends on the surplus-value it produces. Lastly, the competitiveness of industries depends much more than in the past on a very costly logistical infrastructure: communication routes, transport, energy and telecommunications networks, efficient administrations and public services, research and training centres—in short, what Marx referred to as the *faux frais* of the economy, which have to be financed out of the surplus-value produced by industry.

If you examine the 'Chinese miracle', you'll find that China's no exception in this regard. The logistical infrastructure and services lag behind the needs of industry; bottlenecks with regard to water, energy and space hobble growth or stifle it altogether; unemployment is rising dramatically, since industrialization has ruined the rural production workshops that provided more than 100 million workers with a living and agrarian concentration is forcing more than 100 million others to flee the countryside. The ILO estimates unemployment rates in the cities at around 20 per cent and the trend is rapidly rising. In fact, Chinese products can equal northern products in quality only if the recourse to abundant, cheap labour gives way, more generally, to computerization and automation, which are labour- and energy-saving, but more capital-intensive. In China, as in India and the West, the post-Fordist growth model enriches around 20 per cent of the population, but around its hypermodern, post-industrial enclaves it generates vast zones of poverty and neglect that are breeding grounds for organized crime and sectarian or religious wars.

'Growth' doesn't provide a way out of the trap of neo-liberal modernization, unless we define what must grow according to fundamentally different parameters or, in other words, unless we define a quite different economy. The United Nations Development Programme Report attempted a redefinition of this kind in 1996. By adding to the usual wealth 'indicators' the population's state of health, its life expectancy, its rate of literacy, the quality of the environment and the degree of social cohesion, one of the poorest areas in GDP terms on the planet, namely Kerala, turned out to be one of the richest.

I shall try to sum up briefly the reasons underlying this paradox. In an economy in which companies are permanently trying to take market share from each other, each tries to reduce its costs by reducing the quantity of labour it employs: it attempts to increase its productivity. Just suppose that, at some given moment, productivity has doubled. Half as much labour is then needed to produce the same volume of commodities. But the *value* of that same volume will tend also to diminish by half and, at a constant rate of exploitation, the volume of profit will tend to fall in the same proportion. The point is that only living labour is capable of creating value; and, above all, only living labour power is capable of creating a value higher than its own or, in other words, surplus-value.[1] This is the source of profit. For the volume of profit not to diminish, the enterprise either has to double the rate of exploitation at a constant level of production, or to double its production at a constant rate of exploitation. In practice, it seeks to combine the intensification of exploitation and increased production, depending on the economic situation.

Hence, for capitalism, growth is a systemic necessity that is totally independent of—and indifferent to—the material reality of what is growing. It is a response to a need of capital. It leads to that paradoxical development which means that, in the countries with the highest GDP, we live increasingly badly while consuming more and more commodities.

On the basis of a historical context (an Arendtian re-reading of labour in the Greek world), you arrive at a distinction between the categories of 'employment' and 'work'. What is the importance of this distinction and what are its consequences?

Work, as we understand it, isn't an anthropological category. It's a concept invented at the end of the eighteenth century. Hannah Arendt reminds us that in ancient Greece, labour referred to those activities needed to support life. There was neither dignity nor nobility to such activities: they were necessities. To labour was to submit oneself to necessity and that submission made one unworthy of participating in public life as a citizen. Work was reserved for slaves and women. It was regarded as the opposite of freedom. It was confined to the private, domestic sphere.

In the eighteenth century, a different conception begins to take shape. Labour begins to be understood as an activity that transforms and dominates nature, not an activity that submits to it. Moreover, the progressive elimination of domestic industries—particularly weavers—by manufactories lends labour the appearance of a social activity, socially determined and divided. Manufacturing capitalism calls for a labour force that provides it with 'labour and nothing more', with labour '*sans phrases*'. Every proletarian is supposedly exchangable for any other. Proletarian labour is seen as totally impersonal and undifferentiated. Adam Smith saw it as the substance common to all commodities, a quantifiable, measurable substance whose quality, crystallized in the product, determined its *value*.

Shortly afterwards, Hegel gives a broader sense to work in itself: it is not the mere expenditure of energy, but the activity by which human beings put the stamp of their minds on matter and, at first without knowing it, transform and produce the world. Between work which, in the economic sense, is a commodity like any other, crystallized in commodities, and work in the philosophical sense, which is an externalization and objectivization of the self, the contradiction must eventually become clear. Work, as capitalism understands it, is the negation of work as philosophy sees it; it is its alienation. Capitalism determines work as something alien, which, for and by itself, it cannot be.

Marx formulated this in the following way: on the one hand, he wrote (in *Wage Labour and Capital*, 1849), 'work is the active expression of the labourer's own life.' On the other,

> [. . .] this *life activity* he sells to another person in order to secure *the necessary means of life*. His

life-activity, therefore, is but a *means* of securing his own existence [. . .] He does not count the labour itself as a part of his life; it is rather a sacrifice of his life. It is a commodity that he has auctioned off to another. The product of his activity, therefore, is not the aim of his activity.[2]

The primary goal of his activity is to 'earn his living', to earn a wage. It is by the wage which is its payment that labour fits as a *social activity* into the fabric of social exchanges of commodities which structure society, and that the labourer is recognized as a social labourer belonging to that society.

But the most important aspect, from the viewpoint of society, the one that justifies our speaking of capitalist society, lies elsewhere. Labour treated as a commodity—employment—renders *labour structurally homogeneous with capital*. Just as the determining goal of capital isn't the product the enterprise puts on the market but the profit which the sale of that commodity enables it to achieve, so the determining goal of the wage-earner is not *what* he produces but the wage that his productive activity brings him. *Labour and capital are fundamentally complicit in their antagonism, inasmuch as 'earning money' is their determining goal.* In the eyes of capital, the nature of production is of less importance than its profitability; in the eyes of the worker, it is of less importance than the jobs it creates and the wages it distributes. For each, *what* is produced is of little significance, provided it brings a return. Both are consciously or otherwise in the service of the valorization of capital.

This is why the labour movement and trade unionism are anti-capitalist only insofar as they question not just wage levels and working conditions, but the purposes of production and the commodity form of the labour that effects it.

In what way is work at the root of the ecological crisis?

Wage labour is not just a way for capital to grow, it is also, in its organization and modalities, a means of dominating the workers. They are divested of their means of labour, dispossessed of the purpose and product of their work and deprived of the opportunity to determine its nature, length and tempo. The only end-goal that lies within their scope is the money they receive in wages and what it can buy for them. Commodity labour engenders the pure consumer of commodities. The dominated worker engenders the dominated consumer, who no longer produces anything he needs. The producer-worker is replaced by the consumer-worker. Being forced to sell the whole of his time—his whole life—he perceives money as the entity that can redeem everything symbolically. If we add that working hours, housing conditions and the urban environment are all obstacles to the flourishing of individual faculties and social relations, and obstacles to the possibility of enjoying one's non-working time, then we can understand why the worker, reduced to a commodity, dreams only of commodities.

The domination that capital exerts over the workers, by forcing them to *buy* everything they need, meets initially with their resistance. It's mainly the necessities of life that they purchase; their consumption is dictated by their vital needs; and their wages give them just enough to live on. They can resist their exploitation only by collective actions and initiatives, if they unite in struggle on the basis of *their shared needs*. This is the heroic age of trade-unionism, of workers' cooperatives and mutual-aid societies, workers' education associations and class unity and belonging.

At that stage, workers' struggles were mainly conducted in the name of the right to a living, demanding a *sufficient* wage to cover the needs of workers and their families. This norm of *sufficiency* was so influential that craftworkers stopped work when they'd earned *enough* to live in a manner to which they were accustomed, and workers paid by their output could be forced to work 10 or 12 hours a day only by reducing their hourly wages.

From 1920 onwards in the United States and after 1948 in Western Europe, basic needs offered capitalism too tight a market to absorb the volume of commodities it was capable of producing. Only if the production of superfluities increased more and more markedly at the expense of necessities could the economy continue to grow, the accumulated capital be valorized and profits reinvested. Capitalism needed consumers whose purchases were motivated less and less by *shared needs* and more and more by *differentiated individual desires*. Capitalism needed to produce a new type of consumer and a new type of individual: it needed individuals who wanted to free themselves, by their consumption and purchases, from the shared norm; to *distinguish themselves* from others and 'stand out from the crowd'.

The economic interest of the capitalists coincided marvellously with their political interests. The individualization and differentiation of consumers made it possible both to expand industry's markets and to undermine the workers' cohesion and class consciousness. These traits induced behaviour and aspirations in them that were akin to those of the 'middle class'. One of the first to pursue this transformation of the working class methodically was Henry Ford.

In his factories, the assembly lines required repetitive, mind-numbing work, bereft of all dignity, but the workers de-skilled by such work received enviable wages. What they lost in terms of occupational dignity they were supposed to gain in terms of purchasing power. Consumption out of need was, at least in part, replaced by 'compensatory consumption'.

The so-called Fordist period, which lasted with various ups and downs from 1948 to 1973, succeeded in combining rising wages, greater social benefits and public expenditure and, above all, increased production and employment. In those years, quasi-full-employment was based on rises in production higher than the level of productivity gains—that is to say, higher than four per cent. Insofar as it brought security of employment and social security, economic expansion served the immediate interests of the working class. With the exception of a minority Left-wing section of the trade unions, the labour movement didn't criticize the nature and orientation of this expansion but called, rather, for it to be speeded up.

However, in a capitalist regime, the sustained expansion of production involves an acceleration of the circulation and accumulation of capital. Fixed capital (invested in material plant) has to be paid off and made to produce a yield quickly, so that the profits can be reinvested in expanding the means of production.

From the ecological standpoint, speeding up the circulation of capital leads to excluding everything that reduces profit in the immediate term. The continual expansion of industrial production thus entails an accelerated pillaging of natural resources. Capitalism's need for unlimited expansion leads it to try to abolish nature and natural resources and replace them with manufactured products, sold at a profit. The genetically modified seeds the giant multinationals are striving to impose on the whole world are a telling example of this. They are aiming to abolish the natural reproduction of certain plant species and those species themselves, to do away with peasant farmers and their food crops—in short, with human beings' capability to produce their foodstuffs for themselves.

The workers and their organizations—that is to say, commodity labour—share the responsibility for this pillage and destruction only to the extent that they defend employment at all costs in the existing context and, to that end, fight everything that reduces economic growth and the financial profitability of investments in the immediate term.

What Marx wrote 140 years ago in the first volume of *Capital* is strikingly relevant today:

> In modern agriculture, as in urban industry, the increase in the productivity and the mobility of labour is purchased at the cost of laying waste and debilitating labour-power itself. Moreover, all progress in capitalist agriculture is a progress in the art, not only of robbing the worker, but of robbing the soil; all progress in increasing the fertility of the soil for a given time is a progress towards ruining the more long-lasting sources of that fertility. The more a country proceeds from large-scale industry as the background of its

development, as in the case of the United States, the more rapid is this process of destruction. Capitalist production, therefore, develops the techniques and the degree of combination of the social process of production only by simultaneously undermining the original sources of all wealth—*the soil and the worker.*[3]

You've demonstrated that, in our society, the major current problem is no longer production, but distribution. How has this change come about and what are your proposals for confronting this new challenge? Mightn't the disconnection between work and income—an idea you've defended—be part of this change?

The answer's quite simple: when society produces more and more wealth with less and less work, how can it make each person's income depend on the quantity of work they perform? This has become an increasingly nagging question since the transition to post-Fordism. The 'IT revolution', initially called the 'microelectronics revolution', has enabled enormous savings in working hours to be achieved in the fields of material production, management, communications, wholesaling and the entire range of office activities. In an initial phase (1975–85), the political and trade-union Left attempted to push through policies for the redistribution of work and incomes, in accordance with the slogan, 'Work less for full employment and a better life.' These policies failed and we have to understand why.

With computerization and automation, work has ceased to be the main productive force and wages have ceased to be the main production cost. The organic composition of capital (that is to say, the ratio between fixed and circulating capital) has increased rapidly. Capital has become the preponderant factor of production. The remuneration and reproduction of material fixed capital and continuous technical innovation in that sphere required financial resources far in excess of labour costs. In fact, labour costs are often less than 15 per cent of total costs at the moment. The distribution between capital and labour of the 'value' produced by enterprises leans increasingly towards the former. And capital is less and less inclined to give in to the demands of organized labour or negotiate compromises with them. Its main concern is that its preponderant position within the process of production should enable it to lay down the law. In short, it is looking for the way to free itself from social legislation and collective agreements, regarded as unbearable straitjackets in a context in which 'competitiveness' on world markets is the prime imperative. Neo-liberal globalization demands that the social legislation which societies had developed for themselves be abrogated by the laws of the market, for which no one can be held responsible. Globalization was promoted with this tacit aim: to enable capital to smash what was seen as the excessive influence the organized labour had acquired during the Fordist period. Employees were to be forced to choose between poorer working conditions and unemployment.

In reality, globalization brought about both unemployment and inferior working conditions. Stable, full-time, fully paid employment became a privilege reserved in the hundred largest North American corporations for 10 per cent of the personnel. Insecure, discontinuous, part-time work on 'flexible' hours is tending to become the rule.

The 'wage-based' society thus went into crisis. In that society, employment had multiple functions. It was the main way of distributing socially produced wealth; it gave access to social citizenship—or, in other words, to the various benefits provided by the welfare state—benefits financed by the partial redistribution of income gained from work and income gained from capital. It effected a certain type of integration in—and membership of—a society based on work and commodities; it was, in principle, to be available to all. The 'right to work' had been written into most constitutions as a political right, a right of citizenship. It is, as a consequence, the whole of society that disintegrates when employment becomes insecure and 'flexible', and the welfare state is dismantled, without any other society or perspective taking the place of that crumbling order.

Quite the contrary, the representatives of capital continue, with cruel hypocrisy, to vaunt the merits of that same employment they are abolishing in enormous quantities, accusing the workers of pricing themselves out of jobs and the unemployed of being lazy, incapable and responsible for their own unemployment. The employers demand an increase in weekly and annual working hours, claiming that, 'in order to defeat unemployment, people must work more', earn less and retire later. However, at the same time big companies are laying off their employees aged 50 or above, in order to 'improve the age profile of their staff'.

Praising the work ethic and the virtues of work in a context of growing unemployment and insecure employment forms part of a strategy of domination: workers have to be encouraged to fight over extremely scarce jobs, to accept them on any terms and regard them as intrinsically desirable, and workers and the unemployed have to be prevented from uniting to demand a different distribution of work and of socially produced wealth. Everywhere the virtues of North American neo-liberalism are invoked, which, by extending working hours, lowering wages, reducing the taxes paid by the rich and by corporations, privatizing public services and drastically cutting unemployment benefits, has achieved higher economic growth than most other northern countries and succeeded in creating more jobs. Didn't this prove that a contraction in the volume of wages distributed, the impoverishment of the great mass of the citizens and the spectacular enrichment of the richest individuals[4] were no obstacle to the growth of the economy—indeed, quite the opposite?

Well, in fact it didn't. The secret of the growth of the United States economy during the 1990s, years characterized by a quasi-stagnation of the European economy, resides in a policy that no other country can afford itself and which, sooner or later, will have fearsome consequences. Like the other northern economies, the United States economy suffers from a shortage of creditworthy demand. However, it alone is capable of offsetting that shortage by allowing itself to accumulate debt or, in other words, by effectively printing money. To prevent creditworthy demand falling and the economy going into recession, the Central Bank encourages households to get into debt with their banks and consume what they hope to earn in the future. It is the growing indebtedness of 'middle-class' households that was and remains the main engine of growth. At the end of the 1990s, each household owed on average as much money as it hoped to earn in the next 15 months. In 1995, households spent 350 billion dollars more than they earned and this consumption, which was not linked to any productive work, was reflected in a deficit of 100 billion dollars a year in the United States current account balance, which rose to 600 billion in 2005. It was entirely as though the United States was borrowing externally what it was lending internally: it was financing a debt with other debts.

By buying overseas 500 billion dollars worth of goods more than they sold, the United States was keeping the world awash with liquidity. Virtually every country in the world competed to sell the Americans more than the Americans bought from them—that is to say, for the 'privilege' of working for American consumers. Far from ever thinking of calling in US debts, America's creditors did exactly the opposite: they returned to the United States what that country was losing, by buying American Treasury bonds and Wall Street stocks.

However, this amazing state of affairs can last only so long as the Wall Street Stock Exchange continues to rise and the dollar doesn't fall in relation to other currencies. When Wall Street goes into long-term decline and the dollar begins to weaken, the fictional character of outstanding dollar balances will become evident and the world banking system will be in danger of collapsing like a house of cards. Capitalism 'is teetering on the edge of the abyss'.[5]

Producing and producing more is not, then, a problem. The problem is to sell what is produced to buyers capable of paying for it. The problem is the distribution of a production that is achieved with less and less labour and that distributes fewer and fewer means of payment in an irregular, inegalitarian way. The problem is the continually growing gap between the capacity to produce and the capacity to sell at a profit, between producible *wealth* and the commodity form, which is the form of *value* wealth must necessarily assume if it is to be able to be produced within the framework of the economic system currently in force.

The solution to the problem cannot be found either in the mere creation of supplementary means of payment or in the creation of a sufficient quantity of jobs to occupy and remunerate the whole of the population that wants to 'work'—which, on a world scale, means almost a third of the planet's potentially active population.

I shall show in a moment that the solution that consists in increasing the population's purchasing power by creating supplementary means of payment shared out among everyone can't be applied within the framework of the existing system. Before that, however, I shall have to demonstrate that the creation of additional jobs in quasi-unlimited quantities, as has been done in the United States in particular, creates

practically no additional wealth at the societal level, al-
though it does procure a—generally low and irregular—income for a large number of workers.

Not every job is 'productive' in the sense that
term possesses in a capitalist economy. Only labour
that valorizes—that is to say, increases—capital, because the person who performs it does not consume
the entire value of what s/he has produced, is 'productive'. The famous 'sources of employment' by dint
of which governments hope to be able to eliminate
unemployment are mostly unproductive jobs in the
sense I have just outlined. This applies particularly to
those personal services which occupy 55 per cent
of the working population of the United States.
According to Edward Luttwak, this '55% of the
working population are salesmen, waiters and wait-
resses, cleaners, domestic servants, gardeners, nannies
and janitors, and half of them are in low-paid precarious employment, more than a quarter are "working
poor", whose income is below the poverty line, even
when they had two or three jobs.'[6]

It is entirely as though the richest 20 per cent were giving work—in their own service—to two or three poor people. But these jobs don't increase the quantity of means of payment in circulation: they don't create value, but consume value created elsewhere. The pay of these service workers comes from the income their clients have derived from productive labour; it is a *secondary income*, a secondary redistribution of a part of primary incomes. This non-value-creating character of personal services—I am referring to their value in the economic sense only, not their use-value or amenity value—has been summed up perfectly by a major American employer. Discussing the argument by certain neo-liberals that growth would be sustained by forcing the unemployed to earn a living selling flowers on streetcorners, shining shoes or selling hamburgers, he concluded: 'You can't run an economy selling hamburgers to each other.'

Most often, service jobs merely transform into paid employment services that people could exchange without paying for them or activities they could just as easily take on themselves. The transformation of these activities into jobs does not save labour time and gains no time at the societal level; it merely redistributes time. The unproductive character of the services bought and sold is reflected at that level.

There is practically no limit to the expansion of this kind of commercial exchange. In his book *World Philosophie* (Paris: Odile Jacob, 2000), Pierre Lévy envisages all forms of social exchange and all interpersonal relations being transformed into business: 'Sexuality, marriage, procreation, health, beauty, identity, knowledge, connections, ideas—we shall be constantly occupied in doing all kinds of business [. . .] The person becomes an enterprise. Families and nations mean nothing any more.' People then spend their time selling *themselves* to each other. They are, all of them, not just salesmen but commodities in search of buyers.

We have to relocate the call for a subsistence income in this context. Its aim isn't to perpetuate the society based on money and commodities or to perpetuate the dominant consumption model of the so-called developed countries. It is, rather, to extricate the unemployed and the insecurely employed from the obligation to sell *themselves*: 'to liberate work from the tyranny of the job' in Frithjof Bergmann's fine phrase. As an article published by one of the most influential associations of the unemployed in France puts it, the subsistence income must 'give us the means to engage in activities infinitely more rewarding than those they try to force upon us,' activities which are both fulfilling for individuals and create intrinsic riches that no enterprise can manufacture, no wage can buy and whose value no currency can measure.

These intrinsic riches are, for example, the quality of the environment, the quality of education, the bonds of solidarity, aid and mutual assistance networks, the extent of shared knowledge and practical know-how, and the culture developed and reflected in the interactions of daily life—all of them things that cannot take commodity form, that are not exchangeable for anything else, that have no price, but each of which has an intrinsic value. It is on these things that the quality and meaning of life depend, the quality of a society and a civilization. They cannot be produced to order. They can be produced only by the very movement of life and of daily relations. Their production requires unmeasured time.

The point of calling for an unconditional social income is to make possible all these free, unprescribed activities on which the flourishing of human faculties and relations depends. Education, culture, involvement in the arts or sports and games and affective relations do not have to *serve some purpose*. They are activities by which human beings produce themselves in the fullness of their humanity and set their humanity as the absolute goal and meaning of their existence. It is only *additionally* that they also increase the productivity of labour: they enable it to become more intelligent, inventive, efficient, more in control of its own collective organization and external effects, and hence sparing of time and resources. The social income will have this result provided that it isn't subordinated in advance to a sequence of predetermined tasks, provided it isn't the *means* for achieving increased productivity. On the contrary, productive activity must be one of the *means* for human fulfilment and not the other way about. It is when it is that it will consume fewest resources and least energy and time.

This conception clearly runs contrary to the dominant conception of economic rationality. It is fiercely combatted by the representatives of capital. In their view, human beings are first and foremost means of production and their education, training and culture should subserve their productive functions. Education and culture must *serve some purpose*, must provide the economy with labour-power adapted for pre-determined tasks.

The directors of forward-thinking companies are fully aware that this instrumental conception of culture has become indefensible and they acknowledge this sometimes by saying that the things that count in the personnel they need are creativity, imagination, intelligence and the ability continually to develop their knowledge. Time spent at work is no longer the measure of their contribution to production. That time is often less than the time they spend outside their work keeping up their cognitive and imaginative capacities through activities that 'serve no purpose', that *are* human fulfilment and produce such fulfilment fully only on condition that they are not subordinated to alien imperatives.

This is the contradiction currently besetting a capitalism that recognizes 'knowledge' and the development of human capacities as the decisive productive force, but can have that force available to it only on condition that it doesn't enslave it. *The right of human beings to exist independently of the 'work' that the economy needs less and less is henceforth the condition on which the development of a so-called knowledge economy depends*, a 'knowledge economy' which, in fact, attacks the foundations of capitalist political economy.

The call for a subsistence income uncoupled from working hours and from work itself is not, then, utopian. On the contrary, it recognizes the fact that 'work', as it has been understood for two centuries, is no longer the main productive force and that the main productive force, living knowledge, cannot be measured with the economy's usual yardsticks, or be paid for according to the number of hours each person deploys it.

Having said this, I don't think that the subsistence income can be introduced gradually and peacefully through top-down reform. As Antonnella Corsani has written, 'above all, it must not be part of a redistributive logic, but part of a subversive logic of radically transcending wealth based on capital and labour.' The very idea of the subsistence income marks a revolutionary break. It forces people to see things differently and, particularly, to see the importance of the wealth that cannot assume the value form—that is to say, the form of money and commodities.

When it's introduced, the subsistence income will be a different money from the kind we use today. It won't have the same functions. It won't be possible for it to serve goals of power and domination. It will be created 'from below', the product of a general groundswell and, at the same time, of networks of what Bergmann calls 'high-tech self-providing' cooperatives, in response to a combination of the different forms of crisis we sense looming: a climate crisis and an ecological crisis; an energy crisis and a monetary crisis as a result of the collapse of the system of credit. We are all potential Argentinians. What follows depends largely on groups and movements whose practices are sketching out the possibilities of another world and preparing the ground for it.

In your latest book (L'Immatériel), *you tackle the theme of 'the weightless or immaterial economy'. In your view, this spells crisis for capitalism. Why do you say this? If we are moving towards a 'knowledge economy', how is it that some material goods still have such importance, as is the case, for example, with oil? And what happens to agriculture, more particularly where subsidies are concerned?*

The expressions 'knowledge economy' and 'knowledge society' have been around for 35 years in the Anglo-Saxon literature. On the one hand, as I've already pointed out, they mean that work—practically all work in every type of production—demands of workers imaginative, communicational and cognitive capacities—in short, it demands the application of a living knowledge they must draw from within themselves. Work is no longer measurable simply by the time you spend doing it. The personal involvement it requires means there is practically no universal yardstick by which to evaluate it. Its immaterial component takes on greater importance than the expenditure of physical energy.

It's the same with the commercial value of products. Their material substance requires less and less work, their cost is low and their price tends, as a consequence, to fall. To counter this downward trend, companies are transforming material products into vehicles for immaterial, symbolic, affective, aesthetic contents. It's no longer their practical value that counts, but the subjective desirability imparted to them by the identity, prestige and personality they confer on their owner or the quality of knowledge that's supposed to have gone into them. You have, then, a very sizeable industry—of marketing and advertising—producing only symbols, images, messages, styles and fashions or, in other words, the immaterial dimensions that will enable the material commodities to be sold at a high price and that will be constantly innovating so as to make current products outmoded and launch new ones. This is also a way of combatting abundance, which lowers prices, and of producing scarcity (the new is always scarce at first), which increases them. Even everday products and foodstuffs, such as dairy products or washing powders, are marketed this way. The logos of the various firms are designed to confer a special quality on their products, making them incomparable with, and unexchangeable for, others. Just as the extent of its immaterial component made work unmeasurable by a universal yardstick, so the importance of the immaterial component of commodities removes them, temporarily at least, from competition by endowing them with symbolic qualities that are beyond comparison and measure.

If you examine the areas of production that have developed most over the last 20 or 30 years, you see the domination of immaterial commodities there too—in particular, music, the image (photography, video cameras, TV sets, VCRs followed by DVDs) and communications (mobile phones, the Internet). The material here is merely a vehicle for the immaterial; only thanks to the latter does it have use-value. It's chiefly immaterial consumption that has allowed the capitalist economy to continue to function and grow.

We have, then, a situation in which the three basic categories of political economy—labour, value and capital—are no longer measurable by a common yardstick. Some 30 years ago, capitalism tried to overcome the crisis of the Fordist regime by throwing itself into the knowledge economy—that is to say, by accumulating living knowledge as capital. In doing so, it created new problems for itself that have no solution within the framework of the system, since it is, in fact, no small matter to transform living knowledge into 'human capital'. Enterprises are incapable of creating and accumulating 'human capital', and incapable also of retaining lasting control of it. Living intelligence, having become the main productive force, is always threatening to slip from their clutches. On the other hand, formalized and formalizable knowledge, which can be translated into software, is reproducible in unlimited quantities at negligible cost. It is, as a result, a potentially abundant commodity, and its abundance causes its exchange-value to tend towards zero. A true knowledge economy would be an economy based on zero-cost exchange and pooled resources, in which knowledge would be treated as humanity's common property. To exploit knowledge and turn it into capital, the capitalist enterprise has to privatize it and render scarce, by private appropriation and copyrighting, what is potentially abundant and free. And this privatization and rarefaction have a very high cost, as the temporary monopoly the firm acquires against equivalent, new knowledge, against imitations and reinventions, has to be protected by locking off the market to potential competitors by marketing campaigns and in-novations outflanking potential competitors.

Knowledge isn't a commodity like any other, and its commercial, monetary value is always an artificial construct. To treat it as 'immaterial capital' and quote it on the Stock Exchange is, in every case, to assign a fictional worth to something that has no measurable value. What, for example, are the capital of Coca Cola, Nike or McDonald's worth? All are firms that possess no material capital, but simply a 'know-how', a com-mercial organization and a brand name of repute. What is even Microsoft worth? The answer depends essentially on the stock-exchange estimate of the mo-nopoly rents these firms hope to obtain. It's said that the collapse of the Nasdaq in 2001 impoverished the world by 4,000 billion dollars. But those dollars only ever had a fictional existence. If the collapse of 'im-material assets' has demonstrated anything, it's essen-tially the intrinsic difficulty of attempting to make immaterial capital function as capital and to make the knowledge economy function as a capitalism.

The absence of an instrument of measurement common to knowledge, immaterial labour and capital, the fall in the value of material products and the artificial increase in the exchange-value of the immaterial invalidate the tools of macroeconomic measurement. Wealth creation can no longer be measured in monetary terms. The foundations of political economy are crumbling. It's in this sense that the knowledge economy *is* the crisis of capitalism. Not by chance have the last few years produced a string of books, both philosophical and economic, stressing the need to redefine wealth. A different economy is beginning to take shape in the heart of capitalism, an economy that reverses the relation between the production of commercial riches and the production of human wealth.

Notes

1 Surplus-value is the value of production a worker achieves in excess of his/her own needs and those of his/her family. It is an 'economic surplus', to use Paul Baran's terminology. The proportion of surplus-value

in the total value produced by a worker is the rate of surplus-value, which measures the rate of exploitation.

2 Karl Marx, *Wage Labour and Capital* (Whitefish, MT: Kessinger, 2004), p. 12. Also available at: www.marxists.org/archive/marx/works/1847/wage-labour/-ch02.htm [Trans.]

3 Karl Marx, *Capital, Volume 1* (London: Penguin Books, 1976), p. 638 (translation modified). Emphasis mine. [A.G.]

4 In the period 1979–94, 80 per cent of wage-earners in the United States suffered reductions in income, while 70 per cent of the additional wealth produced, thanks to growth, in this same period was monopolized by five per cent of the richest Americans.

5 See Brenner, 'New Boom or New Bubble?' Kurz, who is probably the best critical theorist of the transformations of capitalism and its present crisis, devotes a substantial section of his latest book, *Das Weltkapital*, to the vital function currently performed by financial bubbles. These form through the speculative inflation of financial assets. The rise in the prices of those assets enables the banks to grant increasing credit to borrowers, and hence to sustain economic activity. The financial bubble is, as Kurz puts it, 'a marvellous machine for creating money.' Every bubble ends up bursting

sooner or later, bringing serial bankruptcies in its wake, unless it is followed very quickly by a new and larger bubble. In this way, the stock-market bubble was followed by the dot.com bubble, and the bursting of that bubble was followed by the current property bubble, which is, according to *The Economist*, 'the biggest of all time'. In three years, it has increased the stock-market value of the property sector from 20 to 60 trillion dollars. No one can predict what will follow. The bigger a speculative bubble, the more it threatens, when it bursts, to bring about the collapse of the banking system and of currencies.

6 Edward Luttwak, *Turbo-capitalism. Winners and Losers in the Global Economy* (London: Weidenfeld and Nicolson, 1998). [I have not been able to locate this passage in the edition Gorz cites and it is, therefore, back-translated here from the French.—Trans.]

A NOTE ON THE TEXTS

'Political Ecology. An Ethics of Liberation' first appeared in *EcoRev*, 21 ('Figures de l'écologie politique') (Autumn–Winter 2005).

'The Exit from Capitalism has Already Begun' first appeared in *EcoRev*, 28 (Autumn 2007).

'Political Ecology between Expertocracy and Self-Limitation' first appeared in *Actuel Marx*, 12 ('L'écologie ce matérialisme historique') (1992).

'The Social Ideology of the Car' was first published in *Écologie et Politique* (Paris: Galilée, 1975).

'Destructive Growth and the Productive Alternative' was first published in *Adieux au prolétariat* (Paris: Galilée 1980).

'Global Crisis, De-growth and the Exit from Capitalism' first appeared in *Entropia*, 2 ('Décroissance et travail') (Spring 2007).

'Wealth without Value, Value without Wealth' first appeared in *Cadernos IHV Ideas*, 31 (São Paulo: Unisinos, 2005).